Mathematics – the First Three Years

W & R CHAMBERS Edinburgh
JOHN MURRAY London
JOHN WILEY New York

A Nuffield/CEDO Handbook for Teachers

Published for the Nuffield Foundation and the Centre for
Educational Development Overseas by W & R Chambers, 11
Thistle Street, Edinburgh ; John Murray, 50 Albemarle Street,
London ; and John Wiley and Sons Inc., 605 Third Avenue,
New York

ISBN 0 550 77060 7 (Chambers)
ISBN 0 7195 2052 5 (Murray)
ISBN MO 471 65189 3 (Wiley)

Library of Congress
Catalog Card No : 73 168554

First published 1970
Second impression 1973

Printed in Great Britain by
Newgate Press Limited
London EC1R 4PD

Foreword

The work of the Nuffield Mathematics Project has aroused interest throughout the world, and the Teachers' Guides for the Project have been well received both in Britain and in other countries. Yet there is a need also for some shorter books presenting the material contained in the Guides in a form and sequence which would enable teachers in developing countries more easily to obtain information on the Project's aims and methods.

To provide for this need, CEDO is producing three handbooks specially for teachers overseas: these distil the content of the publications of the Nuffield Project, while preserving its essential aims. They are intended to show ways in which the methods of Nuffield mathematics can be applied with profit in primary schools everywhere — irrespective of the particular syllabus being followed. It would, of course, have been quite impossible to replace the examples and illustrations by material suitable for all overseas countries, for every country must develop its own material from its own environmental sources.

The first of these handbooks, *Mathematics: The First Three Years*, considers the development of a child's awareness of mathematics during the pre-school years and during the first three years' work in the primary school.

Some teachers may find these handbooks sufficient to meet their needs; others will wish to supplement them later on with the full Teachers' Guides. In either case the value of the books will be greatly increased if they are used in conjunction with pre-service and in-service teacher-training courses.

It is the hope of the Nuffield Foundation and CEDO that these books will inspire all those concerned with education to help more young children in every country to gain understanding of mathematics through discovery and first-hand experience.

Clifford Butler
Director of the Nuffield Foundation

Contents

A note on metric units

When the Nuffield Mathematics Project produced its first Teachers' Guides, nearly all English-speaking countries were using the traditional British measures for the affairs of everyday life. Metric measures had been adopted internationally for scientific purposes and for some industries but the measures a child would see in use around him would usually be the yards, miles, pounds, ounces, pints, etc., familiar to his parents. These, therefore, were the units taught in primary schools; metric units were introduced to children much later as a special system used by scientists and also in some foreign countries.

Recently there has been a strong movement to establish metric units for general use. In some countries the change-over to metric units for all aspects of trade and industry has been completed; in others the change is proceeding gradually towards completion by a given date; in a few territories, a decision to change has not yet been finally taken.

The consequent procedures in schools differ as widely. In many primary schools children learn the traditional measures first, use them for their own measuring and learn the numerical skills which the non-metric units demand. In some schools, however, the adoption of the metric system has been complete.

While there is such variation in school programmes it seems best to retain both traditional and metric systems in these handbooks. If a teacher finds that the handbook describes in terms of un-familiar traditional units an activity she wishes the children to carry out, she can readily modify the units in one of the following ways. She can treat the given unit (spoken of as 'the unit') as she would such arbitrary units as cupfuls or handspans and can let the children substitute for it the standard unit that they think suitable. In other conditions she could simply replace the un-familiar unit with the metric unit nearest to it in value, e.g. 7 metres for 7 yards, or 5 half-kilograms for 5 pounds. Sometimes it would be more accurate to convert the measurement to metric units by using an approximate equivalent such as $2\frac{1}{2}$ cm for an inch or $1\cdot6$ kilometres for a mile. The choice depends on the need to keep the final numbers easy to manipulate.

If a diagram shows traditional measurements, the children can measure the given lengths in metric units and can round them off if necessary; for example, $1\cdot5$ inches is measured as $3\cdot8$ cm. Such changes in measuring units may alter the numerical work required but it is important for children to realise that the basic mathematics remains unchanged.

Part I
Pre-school experience

The world of mathematics is one of abstractions largely concerned with symbols. These symbols have been and are being invented by man to help him discover, discern and record the structures, patterns and relationships within the universe.

This great universe seems utterly remote from the small world of the pre-school child, the world of home, garden, family and neighbourhood, the world of things that can be seen, heard, smelt, touched and tasted. Yet if we are to consider the developmental process within which a child begins to perceive the patterns and relationships of mathematics, we cannot ignore the early years.

Early experiences will be outlined under four headings:

A Experience with materials - separate and continuous;
B Experience of space, shape and size;
C Experience of containing, matching and measuring;
D Experience of number words and symbols.

All these experiences can and should lead to the all-important growth of language.

One cannot over-emphasise the importance of pre-school experience. Throughout their education children draw upon resources gained through previous experience to enable them to assess a new situation or tackle a new problem. Language has its roots in the early home environment. We are beginning to realise more fully how much a child's intellectual growth depends on the language used in the home. It is impossible to lay down any programme in this field for a child of any given age, but it is vital to realise that we can only develop what is there already and build on what has gone before.

The early development of ideas is shown in this diagram:

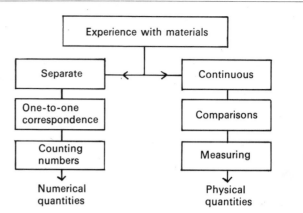

Vocabulary develops hand-in-hand with ideas.

Effective development will depend on:
1 the quality of the experience;
2 the availability of a companion and particularly an understanding adult with whom to talk;
3 the quality of the language used.

A Experience with materials – separate and continuous

A young baby is able to grasp small things, and, largely by trial and error, transfer an object to his mouth. At this stage his mouth is all-important. The object may be his own fist, his mother's finger, part of her necklace that he has managed to grasp, or some toy that he can reach. Coloured beads on strong elastic thread stretched between two supports offer endless possibilities. They feel hard, unlike most other things a baby touches. They move. They can be pushed along, or turned round. And they don't all do it at once. The beads in contact with the baby's hand can be moved about while the others remain in the same position. The string of beads is composed of separate items ('discontinuous').

The child of two, three or four years comes in contact with different materials throughout his waking day. He will learn to recognise them in different ways in different situations, e.g. how the material feels, or 'what I can do with the material'.

He has a box of bricks or blocks. These can be emptied on to the floor, and are then seen as separate items. They can next be built up vertically to form a tower. It soon becomes too tall and rather unsteady, and eventually topples to the ground. The bricks are again seen clearly as separate items.

Alternatively, the bricks can be assembled in a long horizontal line, and pushed along as an imaginary train. The train bumps into another object, perhaps a chair, and disintegrates. Again the separate items are distinguishable.

Outside is a puddle of water. There seems no connection between this and the water in a bowl — yet they both behave in the same way. The child hits the water in the bowl and it makes a lovely splash. He strikes a puddle, with the same result.

After the tower of bricks has tumbled, the separate bricks are clearly seen. The child may refer to *a lot of bricks* and in this instance he is manifestly dealing with 'separate items'.

After the splash in the puddle — a puddle of water remains. Although the child may refer to *a lot of water*, in this instance the content of the puddle is not separate items but a 'continuous' stream.

B Experience of space, shape and size

From the age of only a few months babies begin to explore the world about themselves. Given a chance they will play with their food and drink, and taste or bang everything within reach.

From this natural curiosity and desire to explore and discover on the sensory level, the child will gradually gain various experiences of spatial relationships, although, until he enters school, these will probably not have been consciously put in his way, or enlarged upon.

A baby left to himself experiments with all available materials. He sucks, grasps, releases, pushes and pulls things. Later he becomes aware of a world beyond his reach. He grasps something, moves his hand beyond the edge of the table, and releases the object. It has disappeared from view — hitting the ground with a thud. Here is the first experience of the law of gravity. It is an incredible piece of experience for the baby, who will go on experimenting, i.e. dropping things over an edge, just as long as someone will retrieve them.

The key to the awareness of *space* is movement. As the child becomes more mobile so his world enlarges. The baby who cannot yet crawl will nevertheless try to move if placed on the floor. This early exploratory movement is almost always circular. For movement to be directional, i.e. from A to B, the motivation must be strong. A young child will struggle to move in a specific direction, either crawling or walking, to reach a desired object or person.

Early experiences of *shape* arise in a variety of situations. A building block is found to be of a very different nature from a ball. Place a building block on the floor and it stays put. Put a ball down and it will probably roll away. You can pile building blocks on top of each other, but you cannot do this with balls. A child allowed to help Mother unpack the shopping will see and handle many different shapes, a large number of them cylindrical and rectangular.

Jigsaw puzzles give specific experience of shapes that fit together, but there are many examples of things that fit inside containers: one bowl fits inside another, the crayons fit into the box (but only if they are put in in the right way).

To gain any understanding of what *size* means to a young child we have to imagine the appearance of, say, a room from the eye-level of a three-year-old. Chairs, cupboards and tables are comparatively enormous. The situation is further complicated by the fact that the child grows. He can now see things on a table that was once above his head.

Fortunately some things remain constant, and he will meet situations that do not vary. He will discover that he can never get that particular toy on that particular shelf, because it is always too big.

Slowly, from everyday-life situations, the child will build up a vocabulary to describe these physical experiences. The very common words 'big' and 'little' will be combined with others to give some idea of amount, e.g. 'big lot of water', 'a little bit of cake'.

However, when the child uses and imitates words during these early years he does not necessarily understand what he is saying. For example, so many words descriptive of amount, size and place are relative as used by the adult but to the child this relative use of big, little, wide, long, high, can be confusing. Often the words will be used more in the nature of a name – the tall cupboard, the high chair.

The fact that language is learned by imitation tends to cause confusion in a young child's mind. Returning to the frequently used 'big' and 'little', the child often describes his environment with these:

> Daddy is big, Mummy is big.
> The stools in our kitchen are big.
> I am little.

These are straightforward ideas in that the people and objects concerned are all big in relation to the child himself, who after all is the central character in his own life during these early years.

Through experience the child must come to understand that the words 'big' and 'little' are used relatively and are not absolutes. The same idea of the relative use of words will apply to the whole range of language which has been referred to in the past as 'number vocabulary' – although it has not concerned, and does not concern, number only – many, few, most, least, high, low, narrow, wide, deep, shallow, tall, short, etc. When the child comes to school our aim should be to give as many and as varied experiences as possible so that the child realises that all these words describe relative size, quantity, proportion and place.

C Experience of containing, matching and measuring

Containers serve different purposes, and these purposes are related to the nature of the substance contained. The young child meets problems concerning containers almost every day. If he knocks the box containing a jigsaw puzzle off the table, he can easily pick up the pieces and return them to the box. If he upsets a jug of water, there are no pieces to pick up. One simply wipes up the water.

He might have milk and biscuits for his lunch. He can hold the biscuit in his hand, but the milk has to be contained in a mug.

Children who are allowed to help Mother with the cooking will have plenty of experience of materials removed from one container to another, mixed together, and transformed by the process of cooking.

Laying the table for a meal provides much experience of matching. A cup goes on a saucer, a knife with a fork. 'A plate for Mummy – one for Daddy – one for me.'

When Mother takes the child to buy new clothes they are matched against him for size. When she knits him a sweater she might match it against him to see if it is long enough. All this is valuable pre-measuring experience.

Some fortunate children still see large scales with pans on each side – weights on one side and potatoes on the other. But with the growth of sale by price rather than by weight (in this era of pre-packed goods), children may rarely have this experience in the normal course of events. They will, however, have experience of balancing by hand.

D Experience of number words and symbols
a Vocabulary

Long before they go to school children come into contact with numbers as names. They see and may recognise numerals, e.g. a number symbol as the name of a bus. The words five, eight, two, etc. form part of their vocabulary almost as soon as they learn to talk.

On buses they will hear 'Two nines, please'.

At home they will hear number words occurring frequently in normal conversation.

Quite soon children learn to recite these words in a particular order – 'One, two, three, four, five, six' – and so on. This is a satisfactory activity in that it seems to delight the adults!

b Folk tales and nursery rhymes

As soon as children are old enough to enjoy traditional stories and nursery rhymes these words appear again, this time involved in fantasy, embodied in the world of nonsense, wonder and magic.

Some words appear regularly, e.g. three and seven.

> The three little pigs.
> The three billy goats gruff.
> Snow White and the seven dwarfs.

The sequence of number words appears in rhymes.

> One, two, three, four, five.
> Once I caught a fish alive.
> Six, seven, eight, nine, ten,
> Then I let it go again.

> One, two, buckle my shoe,
> Three, four, knock at the door,
> Five, six, pick up sticks,
> Seven, eight, lay them straight,
> Nine, ten, a big fat hen.

There seems to be very little difficulty concerning this aspect of vocabulary growth. These number words arise naturally and in a variety of contexts.

We are, however, a long way from establishing a notion of number, and thereby making these words meaningful.

c Number symbols
Some children will be able to identify the symbol on the front door of their home at a very early age. Home is very important to a young child, and this symbol on the front gate identifies this place as 'mine'. If the symbol is a simple shape such as a seven, the young child may even be able to reproduce it.

7

Obviously the child who lives at number five hundred and sixty-two will have far more difficulty both in remembering the sounds that make up the words and identifying the complex sequence of shapes which form the symbol.

562

Number symbols, or numerals, are all around us and it would be a mistake to suppose that children first meet them in school. It would also be a mistake to suppose that they are as yet meaningful to the child in a mathematical sense.

Summary
The background of experience of the child determines the starting point when he comes to school. If he has not been fortunate enough to have enjoyed a rich and varied set of activities in these early years, if he has not been able to discuss these with someone who uses language with flexibility and imagination, then these opportunities must be made available in school as a first priority, for on such a foundation does his future development depend.

Part II
Before counting or measuring

1 Background to activities in school

If a child has had very little experience with material, the play and free experiment stage will have to be experienced sooner or later.

At five this may take several months but at the age of eight it may take only days. The activities covered in this book are those most often found in schools, but it is hoped that the teacher will be able to apply the same approach to other situations which are not dealt with here. Many of these activities were provided in the first instance to give very young children a rich and stimulating environment in which they could develop socially, emotionally, physically and intellectually. Because the primary motive was not intellectual, the attitude 'as children grow older they do not need to play' still prevails, but many teachers have realised through their own experience that more learning and indeed more enjoyable learning can be gained by working through the interests of children and many of these interests do, in fact, arise during play.

During the early stages free play is desirable with as much variety of equipment as possible within any basic activity. This is necessary because, although a child may be developing well in one direction, in another there may be difficulties. Through these activities children are gaining physical skills – the ability to use hand and fingers with control and to co-ordinate sight and touch with thought and speech. They need to be able to pour water without spilling it, to build and balance bricks easily, to fit shapes together.

A child's seeming misuse of material may be due to physical control but is more often the result of an emotional problem. The child who throws sand, who squirts water over everyone, who delights in destroying other children's models and drawings is often responsible for these activities being denied to a class on the grounds that 'the children get nothing from them, they just mess about'. But many children have no need to 'play out' difficulties and, given a challenging environment and situations carefully structured by the teacher, they will begin to experiment and discover on their own initiative. To get the maximum amount of satisfaction and learning out of practical situations each activity needs to have its range of stimuli varied and extended regularly.

2 Experience of relations

The word 'relations' probably brings to mind members of a family – parents, aunts, grandfathers, nephews, and so on. It could be stated that John is the son of Mr Smith.

'Is the son of' expresses the relationship of John to Mr Smith.

Another familiar example of a relationship is that of equality,

$$3 \times 2 = 6,$$
$$3 + 2 = 5.$$

The 'relation' reads 'is equal to'. But is this particular relationship as easy and straightforward as it seems? Do children always really understand when they write down a 'sum'?

Perhaps in the past we have taken too restricted a view of mathematics for young children, even regarding it as a concentrated dose of 'arithmetic' which somehow has to be swallowed. And so a wider (even, it is hoped, simpler) study is being made here so that the familiar processes will be widely and firmly based and really understood. We begin, therefore, with a variety of relationships between two different objects, for example:

Here the black ribbon is *longer* than the white ribbon; the white ribbon is *shorter* than the black ribbon. It is helpful from the beginning to look at a situation in different ways. The black ribbon is *narrower* than the *white* ribbon. The white ribbon is *wider* than the black ribbon.

By making such comparisons the child's powers of observation are being developed. He is learning to look closely at materials and, in determining their similarities and their differences, he is in effect defining relations.

Children need a great deal of experience in the comparisons that can be made between two separate objects, for example, two tins, bricks, sticks, parcels, bottles, lids, before proceeding to a more complex situation.

the bat *belongs* to Peter

the ball *belongs* to Jane

Here we have a boy, a girl, a bat, and a ball. The boy and girl are both children. The bat and the ball are both toys. The relation is between children and toys.

Peter has a bat.
Jane has a ball.

The relation between Peter and the bat is the same as that between Jane and the ball.

Many ordinary classroom experiences can be described and even recorded specifically to show a relation.

Here the relation 'played a' existed between some children and percussion band instruments. It would probably not be recorded in this way, a less permanent record being more suitable. Another way of recording the same information would be to have cards bearing the children's names pinned on one side of a display board and pictures (or names of the instruments) on the other side. The relation could then be shown by ribbons or strings.

When permanent recording includes the use of the arrow, then the way in which the arrow is being used must be clearly defined. In the example above it was defined as indicating

played a

The recording then makes sense, and can be easily translated into words. For example:

Peter played a triangle.
Tony played a tambourine.

The arrow is clearly seen as a shorthand symbol, a quicker way of recording the relation.

Particular kinds of relations such as ordering relations and equivalence relations will be considered later.

3 Early experiences of sorting

Early experiences of sorting are usually associated with tidying up. A selection of items picked up from the classroom floor, for example, pieces of jigsaw, building blocks, crayons and paper, all need putting away, and the children will find the right place to put them. The paper will be put in the wastepaper basket, the crayons in the crayon tin, the jigsaw pieces in their appropriate boxes and the building blocks in the brick box.

Sorting out the classroom junk box will involve putting tins, boxes, jars, corks, lids, fabrics and string in their appropriate places. Tidying the Home Corner will involve sorting out dolls' clothes, bedding, tea things, cleaning things, and so on. All these are early experiences of classifying, sorting things according to some determined common factor, perhaps differentiating between tins and boxes, although on another occasion they may

This is a banner on which are ten squares (all of different colours) each having attached to it by string a rectangular strip of the corresponding colour. Each strip fits into a slot in a circular disc on the banner, again in the corresponding colour. This has been used to help small children in a nursery class in identifying and matching colours: there is a one-to-one correspondence between the squares and the discs with the corresponding colour. The relation is *has the same colour as* and is shown by the strings.

all be classified as containers; differentiating between dolls' clothes and dolls' bedding, although on another occasion these may all be classed as 'things that belong to our dolls'.

The teacher should take full advantage of these everyday occurrences by talking with the children and by helping them to describe their experiences and to explain why they are sorting things in a particular way.

'Those are all dolls' clothes and these are all sheets and blankets and things like that.'

Some teachers find it helpful to provide a specific piece of equipment in order to foster this kind of work, for example, a bag of oddments, or perhaps a large well-partitioned box supplied with a variety of odds and ends.

Possible items for the sorting box are:

buttons	beans
shells	screw tops from bottles or tubes
matchboxes	corks
pebbles	cotton reels

The children might sort like this:

and then later perhaps group together buttons, shells, boxes:

On p. 9 we see how a collection of animals was sorted by a six-year-old into categories. It is not clear why there are two separate lots of birds, but the lower set may be fishes.

At other times the children will, with encouragement, sort a collection according to many different criteria, e.g. according to

colour
texture
shape
things that have holes in and those that don't
things from the beach, from trees, from shops, and so on.

The idea of a set

A very young child will get hold of Mother's handbag and empty it onto the floor. This is a more mathematical activity than may appear at first sight. Left alone with a jumble of objects, children will investigate and begin to sort and classify. It is simpler to refer to a 'jumble of objects' as a set. The criterion for a set is really simple; it is for our purposes sufficient to say that a collection is called a set if it is clear that any given one of the objects really does belong to the collection.

These may be listed as lipstick, pen, purse, diary, scissors, compact. They may be rearranged but they would still be the 'same' set, as a set is completely determined by its 'elements', that is, the objects in the set. It is necessary to be able to tell whether any given object is a member of the set or not.

A policeman who emptied Mother's handbag onto a table would be in serious trouble if he could not tell whether a hand grenade on the table came from the handbag or not. It would not be enough for him to show that he could distinguish the hand grenade from the lipstick. What matters is which set it belonged to: the set of things in the handbag or the set of things previously on the table.

A collection of animals is sorted by a 6-year-old into categories (it is not clear why there are two separate lots of birds).

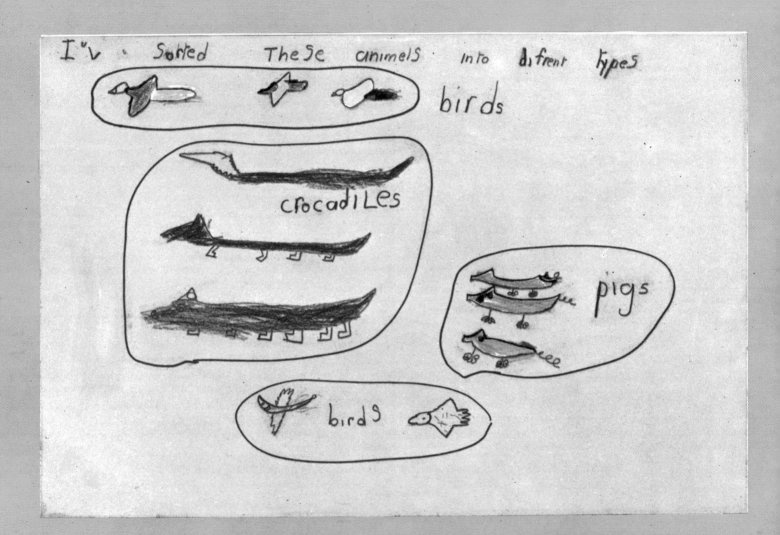

The number of elements in a set is a much later idea and the fact that there is the same number even if the contents are moved round is even more sophisticated. We return to this later.

To lead on to this idea of a set, a sorting box may contain one each of, say, a piece of string, a penny, a length of ribbon, a cotton reel, a button, and a ball of wool.

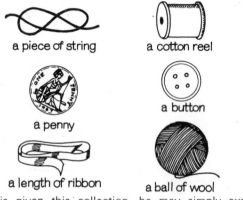

a piece of string

a cotton reel

a penny

a button

a length of ribbon

a ball of wool

If Peter is given this collection, he may simply explore the materials by feeling them, or separate them into categories:

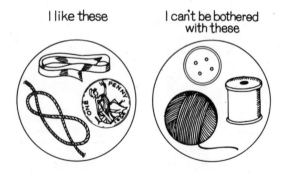

I like these

I can't be bothered with these

Of course Peter would not label them or wrap them up like this; this is simply a mathematical representation to show what has happened.

Every opportunity should be taken to start a discussion. For example, Peter might select two of the things he likes and say:

'This one is bigger than that one' or
'This one is softer than the other one'.

In fact what Peter has done is to start with a set of objects (the contents of the box) and split it up into sub-sets, consisting of (i) the things he likes and (ii) the things he cannot be bothered with. He has made a partition of the set; each object belongs to just one of the sub-sets.

With young children who are busy sorting, the opportunity can be taken to foster discussion, leading to remarks such as the following:

'All those are white.'
'All these are pink.'

'This one is the same colour as that one.'
'Tiger is the same colour as Bear.'

'Jane's dress is the same colour as mine.'
'My dress is the same colour as Penny's.'

'Has the same colour as' is a relation. Other relations such as 'is longer than' will also arise naturally. Many opportunities arise in the classroom for general sorting out, classifying and reclassifying. For example, children frequently experiment with a variety of objects in a water tray to find out whether the objects float or sink. Some children had as a particular set of objects: cork, nail, safety pin, pencil, bead, pebble, shell, button, cotton reel, penny. They sorted them according to whether the 'elements' of the set (cork, nail, etc.) float or sink.

Things that float	Things that sink
cork	nail
pencil	safety pin
bead	pebble
cotton reel	shell
	button
	penny

'Partitioning' consists of splitting a set into 'sub-sets' such that each sub-set contains at least one element and each element belongs to just one sub-set. It is easy to see what this is all about if you translate it back in terms of the children's collection. They simply sorted the set into two heaps, which could be labelled 'float' and 'sink'. There is at least one element of the set in each heap, each element is in one of the heaps, but no element can belong to more than one (either it floats or it sinks).

Here the children have removed all the items from the water tray and placed them on a table. A hoop is used to enclose them and a stick is placed across the hoop.

Other forms of recording:

(a)

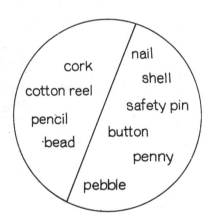

(b)

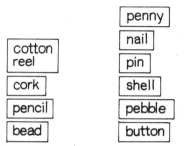

things that float   things that sink

Here the recording suggests a block graph.

(c)

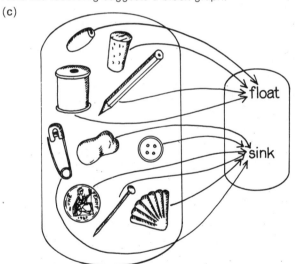

The experiment concerned what happened to objects when they were placed in water. In (c) this relation was denoted by an arrow indicating: *'placed in water, will'*.

The information was then quite clear.

A cotton reel, *placed in water, will* float.
A penny, *placed in water, will* sink.

(d) The next way shows the relation as a set of 'ordered pairs'. The information can be shown in full as:

(cork, float)
(bead, float)
(pencil, float)
(cotton reel, float)
(nail, sink)
(pin, sink)
(shell, sink)
(pebble, sink)
(button, sink)
(penny, sink)

As an example of the relation *placed in water, will*, we can take cork as a first member and read

Cork, *placed in water, will* float.

This method of recording offers an early opportunity of finding out that the order in which one puts things is important.

(float, cork)

is obviously silly. Children can have fun turning things round to see if they still make sense.

(e) Here the information is recorded in the kind of chart usually called a table:

	float	sink
cork	x	
nail		x
cotton reel	x	
pin		x
shell		x
pebble		x
penny		x
pencil	x	
button		x
bead	x	

It is not suggested that every investigation should be recorded in all these ways. In many instances it will be inappropriate to record at all. Moreover, some of these forms of recording are more complex than others. The examples have been included to enable teachers to be aware of the wide range of possibilities that exist, all of them laying foundations for later development in mathematics.

The illustration, 'Dinner chart for Friday', (p. 13) shows a set of children, aged five, partitioned into 'those who stay for dinner' and 'those who go home for dinner'.

4 Development of sorting

Sorting is a natural activity which children enjoy. It is also a necessary stage towards understanding the meaning of number. In addition to this, the notions introduced lead later to further logical thought and decision-making.

We have so far dealt with a single partition of a set into two sub-sets (e.g. float, sink). Later, sets may be partitioned into more than two sub-sets. For example,

Jill has a well-defined set of objects: she knows the elements which make up the set and can easily distinguish between them.

Jill's set of toys

She might split them up, or *partition* the set, according to whether the 'elements' (in this case, the toys) are (i) animals, (ii) dolls or (iii) cars.

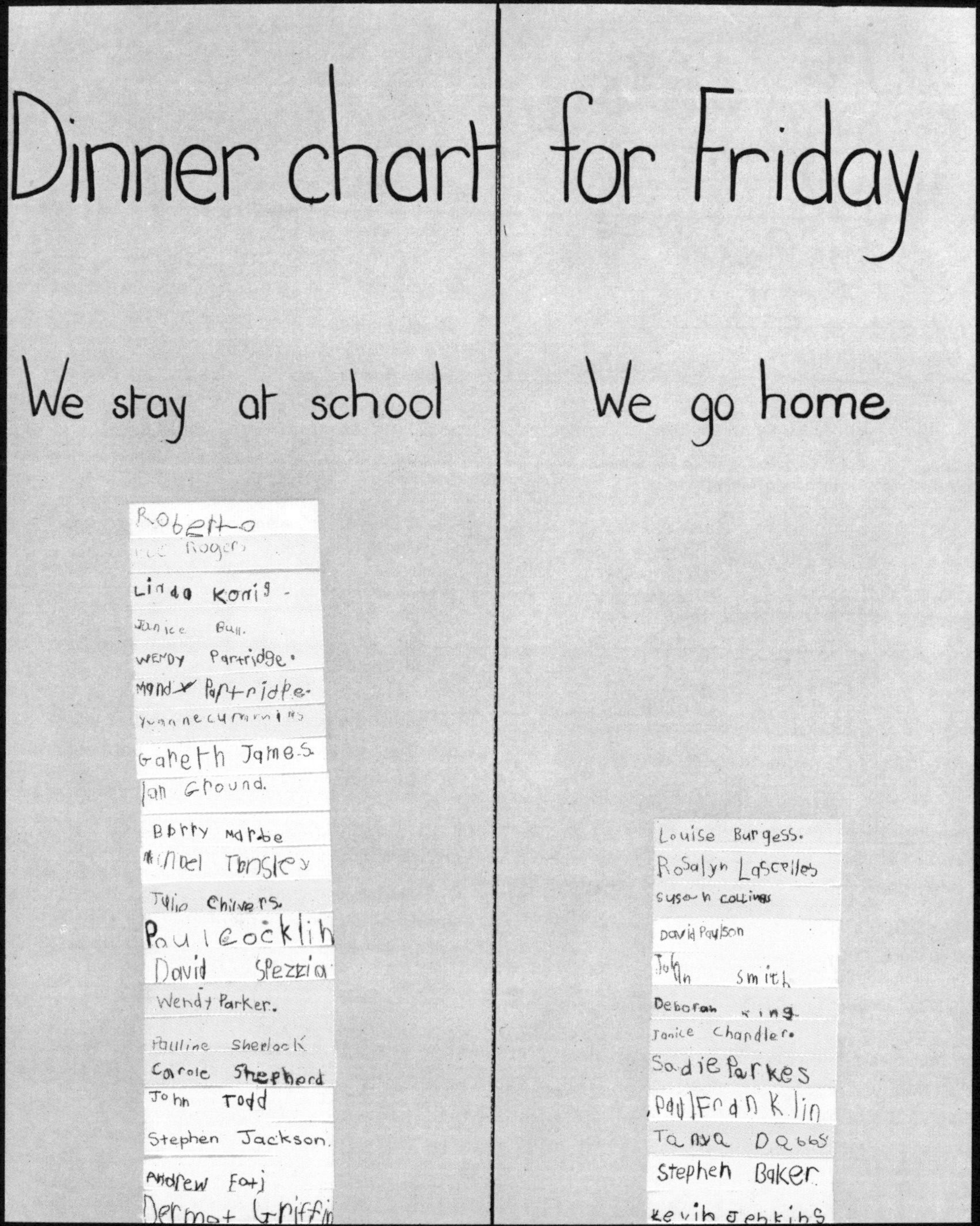

Dinner chart for Friday

We stay at school

Roberto Rogers

Linda Konig.

Janice Bull.

Wendy Partridge.

Mandy Partridge.

Yvonne Cummins

Gareth James.

Ian Ground.

Barry Marbe

Michael Tansley

Julia Chivers.

Paul Cocklin

David Spezzia

Wendy Parker.

Pauline Sherlock

Carole Shepherd

John Todd

Stephen Jackson.

Andrew Foti

Dermot Griffin

We go home

Louise Burgess.

Rosalyn Lascelles

Susan Collins

David Paulson

John Smith

Deborah King

Janice Chandler.

Sadie Parkes

Paul Franklin

Tanya Dobbs

Stephen Baker

Kevin Jenkins

To take another example, suppose a set of children is partitioned:

		Others (i.e. those
Blue eyes	Brown eyes	with neither blue
		nor brown eyes)

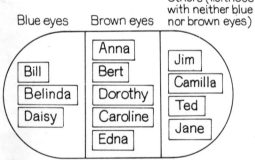

They are sorted into three 'sub-sets' according to whether they have

a blue eyes: Bill, Belinda, Daisy,
b brown eyes: Anna, Bert, Dorothy, Caroline, Edna,
c eyes neither blue nor brown: Jim, Camilla, Ted, Jane.

Partitioning often involves a subjective decision, e.g. are Hazel's eyes blue, brown or neither? The decision need not objectively be 'correct' — it will serve the purpose.

The idea of sorting can be extended further. For example, children taken for a nature walk in the spring will no doubt return with armfuls of specimens. The first classifications would probably be between flowers, leaves, stones, moss, and so on. The flowers might be sorted out according to their known names:

primroses windflowers
violets celandines
bluebells

They might be sorted out according to colour:

yellow flowers
white flowers
blue flowers

At a later stage children would be able to make more complex classifications and produce something like the following table:

	no scent	scent	smooth stem	hairy stem
primrose	x			x
violet	x		x	
bluebell	x		x	
wood anemone		x		x
celandine		x	x	
lords and ladies		x	x	

We have now expressed two relationships, (i) between the flowers and their 'scentedness' and (ii) between the flowers and their type of stem.

Another way of representing these relationships is to make loops of string or wool and put the flowers in the appropriate loops. For example, it might be decided that all the scented flowers should be put in a particular loop.

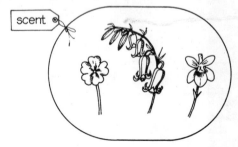

(Note that in this sequence of diagrams the tabs with words inside are meant to represent labels tied to the loops.)
Or again the smooth-stemmed flowers might be put together.

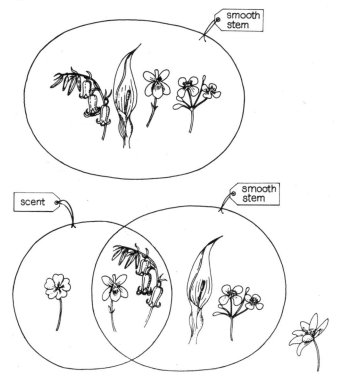

Here the violet and bluebell will have to be put in the overlapping part or *intersection*; they must be in the 'scent' loop, but they must also be in the 'smooth stem' loop. The wood anemone must be put somewhere outside, having neither scent nor smooth stem.

Displays of information using different loops to show different categories are called Venn diagrams. These have many uses, for example, in fostering the beginnings of logical argument.

The children themselves can take part. For instance, suppose there are five children: Jack, Jill, Ben, Julie, Diana; they are selected if they are 'girls' or 'curly-headed' and actually put in the appropriate loops. The pattern might turn out like this:

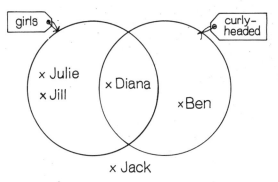

This would show that Diana is both a girl and curly-headed, while Jack is neither. It can also be seen, for example, that Jill is not curly-headed.

For Katie, Sheila, Jane, Mark, John the pattern might have been this:

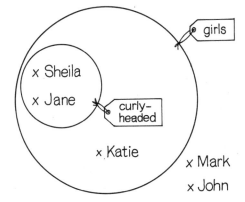

From this pattern, we could deduce that in our new collection of children all the curly-headed ones are girls since the set of 'curly-headed' is included in the set of 'girls'.

Representation in the form of a table, e.g. Jill's toys (p. 12).

	doll	animal	car
Andy	x		
Cindy	x		
Rabbit		x	
Dog		x	
Cat		x	
Sports			x
Mini			x

gives a preview of how a mathematician might record the same information:

	doll	animal	car
Andy	1	0	0
Cindy	1	0	0
Rabbit	0	1	0
Dog	0	1	0
Cat	0	1	0
Sports	0	0	1
Mini	0	0	1

Here 1 means *is* (Rabbit *is* an animal) and 0 means *is not* (Rabbit *is not* a doll or a car).

Our development so far will lead on to consideration of the number of elements in each set (How many girls? How many curly-headed girls? and so on). Children will probably be able to count up to 2 or 3 before they come to school, but there will be sets with more elements than this. We are therefore ready to turn to the business of beginning to understand number. (See p. 35.)

5 Experimental and creative activities

a Sand play

Free play with a wide variety of materials is needed to lay the foundations of measuring. Each class could have a large tray of *coarse sand*, sometimes allowed to become completely dry so that some experience will be gained of the properties of the wet and dry material. An old water tray, zinc bath or wooden tray (perhaps 18 in by 24 in), which would fit on a table and which could be shared between classes, could be used for *silver sand*.

Buckets, tins, plastic cups, mugs, beakers, washing-up liquid containers cut open in various ways, spades, rakes, ladles, spoons,

sieves of all shapes and sizes can be provided. When sand is being used dry, funnels or containers with lips and handles help the children to pour.

Vocabulary and points to bring out of the play

One vocabulary will be concerned with the shape and size of the containers and the various relationships between them; another will be concerned with the sand itself.

i Containers

Wide, narrow, thin, thick, tall, short, deep, shallow, round (later circular, curved), flat, straight, how many, how few, full, empty. Children will undoubtedly use big, bigger, biggest, bigger than, small, smaller than, smallest, but the teacher should encourage them to explain what they mean: for example, on a particular occasion when the child says 'bigger' he may mean 'holds more than', 'weighs more than' or even possibly 'is longer than'.

The children may be led to notice the differences and similarities between the look of a container and the shape 'inside'. For example, a round tin will make a round sand pie. Young children often make symmetrical patterns with sand pies, and although no observations may come from the children at this stage, it is useful for the teacher to have a knowledge of symmetry when patterns are being made in the sand and a variety of differently shaped containers are being used (see p. 131).

ii The sand

How much, how much more, how much less, all leading to the use of the word 'amount' (volume of sand).

The frequent complaint — 'there isn't enough sand' — can lead to discussion about the situation. Should more sand be added, or a smaller share be given to each child, or should fewer children play with the existing quantity?

While the children are playing, the teacher will be able to observe them matching, sorting and counting in many situations. From the very beginnings of play with sand and buckets and tins, children are having the experience of filling three-dimensional space, leading eventually to the concept of volume.

After considerable free play a point to bring out is the comparison of size between two containers — which holds the more sand? Even at an early stage the children can be asked to guess or estimate the answer before discovering for themselves. Some children seem to find the comparison easier by filling the containers with spoonfuls of sand and comparing the numbers needed rather than pouring from one to the other, but this may be the result of insufficient experience of matching and comparison. A pair of scales will give children extra opportunities for discovery. A crude balance made by the teacher would be sensitive enough for this purpose; indeed, sand might well damage new and expensive apparatus. Teachers will probably find that taking balances to the sand, rather than sand to the weighing table, will be a more practical proposition, especially with younger children. Children who have had much experience of filling containers by various means (cups, spoons, scoops, shovels full) might suggest weighing the sand in each container as a quicker method of finding which contains the more. This will lead to extra vocabulary: heavy, light.

Three or four boxes of various shape and size, a spoon or some scales, and a tray of silver sand will provide much thought and experiment for children at later stages of sand play.

Even at this stage children may discover that two containers of different shape will hold the same quantity of sand — an important experience leading towards the concept of invariance of volume when position or shape is changed. If the children are on the way towards establishing the concept, they will be able to answer the question: 'If the two boxes hold the same amount of sand, what can you say about the amount of space inside each of them?'

If a child does not understand this question, then much more experience of filling and emptying of containers is necessary, not only with sand but in other ways to be outlined in subsequent sections. Also it will be necessary to find time to talk about what the children are doing as they play, to make sure, for instance, that they understand what we mean by the size and shape of a container, and what we mean by its capacity: the amount of space inside it.

Of course, the teacher wishing the children to make discoveries will ensure that there really are some tins in the sand tray which, although of different shape, do hold just about the same amount; that is, the situation will be arranged to allow the children to discover something. The teacher's observation, insight and skill will play an important part in the children's success, and must continually be used in conjunction with provision of material.

b Water play

The most valuable equipment is a range of containers of all shapes and sizes, plastic and rubber tubing, sieves, colanders and strainers, jugs, funnels, small corks and sponges, very large stones and small pieces of wood.

The children will be filling containers with water, as they did with sand, and from a carefully planned set of equipment will be gaining experiences of volume and capacity. More can be seen if some of the items are made of transparent material — for very young children glass is not always advisable; young children find a short length of tubing easier to cope with than a long piece.

Teachers will find that the gradual introduction of equipment needing a greater degree of physical skill will be most satisfactory. The addition to the water of non-toxic detergent, or alternatively dye or paint in small amounts, will stimulate any flagging interest. As with all children's play there will be many opportunities at the water tray to count, match and sort. It is useful sometimes to suggest a change of equipment from water to sand tray, and vice-versa, so that children can find out for themselves why certain items (funnels, tubing, scoops, sieves) are used with one material and not with another.

Vocabulary and points to bring out
All the language descriptive of shape and size of container noted in the last section on sand will be used in this activity.

The characteristics of liquids which are within a child's own experience may be discussed: how a liquid has to be contained in something, what happens when a liquid is spilled, poured, heated, frozen, etc., how it takes the shape of a vessel used, how water can be made into a jet, a spray, or a fountain. A five-year-old standing by the water tray said, 'If I get in our baby's bath the water comes over the top'. Such a natural observation will often begin a whole train of experiment, discovery and discussion.

Teachers will find that the children will need some help at first to decide on what they really mean by 'full', and much practice is needed to gain the physical skill by which a young child can obtain the required amount of liquid. Discussion about how milk and lemonade bottles are 'filled' and the amount of space left at the top, will help the children to realise from the very beginning the approximate nature of measurement. The children will be using the language of measurement in their play long before they understand the implications of the words they are using. At 5 and 6 children will refer to *any* quantity of water, during their play, as being a 'pint' or a 'gallon'; but there is a danger at this stage in attempting to teach standard measurement just because children are heard to be using words wrongly. (The approach to standard measurement is dealt with on pp. 55 ff.)

From the point of view of mathematical concepts, water play is important in establishing a basis of experiences which will lead to the eventual and true understanding of volume and capacity. The children will be filling three-dimensional space and discovering relationships between containers.

The next discovery is reversibility. If water from a full jug is poured (carefully) into another container, the process is reversible: that is, the water can be poured back again and the jug will again be full. This is a large step towards understanding the *invariance of volume*; that is, appreciating that no matter how the water (or other incompressible material) is moved about, the amount of it remains constant.

c Picture, pattern and model making
This section refers to painting, drawing, woodwork, the making of collages, the construction of models in all media: paper, clay, Plasticine, dough, wire, papier-mâché.

Although many teachers may arrange these activities for purely creative purposes, much incidental mathematical experience may arise from them. The language used while engaged on a particular piece of work, and the children's and teacher's observations on various aspects, will help to heighten the awareness of shape, pattern and size in the environment.

These activities fall roughly into two categories:

i the painting and drawing of pictures and patterns, when children are covering surface·

ii model making, when children are working·in three dimensions (for young children, collages are another form of picture making).

i Picture and pattern making
Experiences which may be gained in this activity are those concerned with area, space, length and measurement.

In making pictures and patterns with paint, crayon, charcoal, chalk, gummed paper, pieces of material, etc., children are covering a flat surface, one of the few times when this arises naturally in the young child's school environment. Young children enjoy 'printing' patterns in various ways: first with their hands, then with sponges or cut potatoes, and later making their own felt patterns for printing. Their first prints are usually random in character, with no order about them, but occasionally a child will at once produce a symmetrical pattern.

Examples of symmetry found in the children's work may be discussed, as from an early age some children produce, quite naturally, stylised and formal patterns which are highly symmetrical in character. This is the prelude to much significant mathematics. (See pp. 136 ff.)

When children have had plenty of experience of printing patterns on rectangular sheets of paper, the shape of the paper can be varied; a square or a circle may provide an interesting stimulus. Also the provision of paper with an existing pattern may produce unusual results; checked or striped wallpaper can be used if not of the washable kind. Practice in, and experience of, arranging shapes in a limited area is gained when working with gummed paper, felt or material. Ideas of length and measurement in their simplest forms grow through the *comparison* and *matching* used by the children to make their pictures and collages from all these materials.

ii Model making

This activity involves experiences of volume, space, substance, length, and, less frequently, area and weight.

While making models, children are concerned with the fitting together of pieces of card, wood, junk material, etc., into three-dimensional shapes. Apart from gaining practice in the quite difficult physical skills needed to cut various materials and fix them together, children may also discover facts about shapes. They find that it is easier to stick two rectangular boxes together than it is to stick a rectangular box to the curved surface of a cylinder or sphere. In doing this they are experiencing the nature of flat and curved surfaces. They find that it is difficult to cover the head or face of the doll that they have made, but easier to cover its arms and legs; when fixing wheels to a car or lorry they find that each pair of wheels must match in size to ensure free running, and that to make the wheel turn properly they need to put the 'axle' (nail or paper fastener) through its centre; they find that a large and heavy box is difficult to stick on top of a small, light one, but that the other way round the task is simpler.

When children are using clay, Plasticine and dough mixture (flour, water, salt) they are gaining experience of a 'continuous', solid quantity. If using a limited amount of these materials, the children will often 'share out' between themselves – as with sand they will say there is not enough, and the possibilities of less clay for each child, more clay being brought to the table, or of fewer children using it, are all mathematical solutions. While using their own individual amount of material the children find that they can make a number of small things, a lesser number of larger things or indeed just one really large model. This again is an experience of quantity and also an experience leading to 'conservation of volume' because although clay, dough, and Plasticine are all slightly compressible, the 'amount' that a child is using, without any being added or any being taken away, remains practically the same.

Vocabulary

'Shape and size' vocabulary will be used during these creative activities, but, in addition, the nature and texture of materials will be observed – whether they are hard, soft, smooth, rough, spiky, tough or easy to cut or tear. Other words defining position in space, or of one object in relationship to another, are frequently used – up, down, across, on top of, underneath (later, over and under) in front of, behind, next to (later, left and right).

d Music, movement and physical education

All young children delight in sound and movement.

Music

Music is now an accepted part of our environment. It blares forth from record player and radio, and may be heard in the background of a department store or railway station. In school, opportunities are provided for making music as well as listening to it, and this affords pleasure to most young children, although their ability to appreciate rhythm and melody as accepted in the music of the western world is largely uncertain in their earliest years.

One of the aims of this work is to help children to be more sensitive to sound – to be aware of the pattern and relationships within it. Young children enjoy clapping their hands to a piece of music; later this can be compared with the tickings or chimes of a clock. The experience is variously described as pulse or time-beat. Mathematically we are concerned here with awareness of a regular interval, in this instance an interval of time.

Chimes of a clock

Experience of regular interval

Percussion bands offer further adventures in this field. Two small units may be realised as being in some way equivalent to a large one.

All music does not, however, involve such regularities, and early experiences also include excursions into what is variously described as pattern or rhythm.

Lavender's   blue dilly dilly   Lavender's   green

It is rhythm or pattern which gives shape and significance to this sequence, yet musically and mathematically there is a three-ness about it which reveals itself on analysis:

This is later referred to as three beats in a bar. None of this analysis is necessary for young children, but through growing awareness of rhythm these patterns and relationships will become meaningful.

Melody offers further experiences of sequences and intervals, most of them irregular in the early years. Young children will come across the words *high* and *low* in connection with notes on a piano or recorder, and enjoy responding to signals of this kind.

Movement
The key to awareness of space is movement. Opportunities are provided in school for young children to experience the joy of moving in as large a space as possible. As children enter the hall or playground for movement they use the available space freely, and frequently move round so as to form a circle.

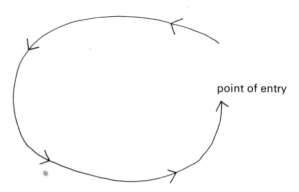

point of entry

A few seconds later it will be seen that the circle is becoming a spiral:

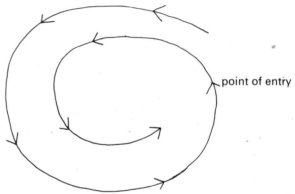

point of entry

The observable floor pattern bears a marked resemblance to children's early drawings, sometimes described as scribbles. Here the circle and the spiral are also clearly apparent. For some time the floor patterns remain predominantly those of the circle and spiral but eventually other possibilities emerge as space awareness develops.

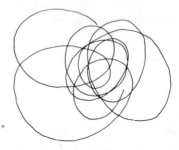

The actual word *space* offers many alternatives. In movement lessons children are sometimes asked to find a space, or to make more use of space. They also hear space used to mean up there — away, beyond — and the adjective outer is frequently applied to it. In spite of this vocabulary difficulty, it seems clear that a great contribution towards the understanding of spatial relationships can be made through experience of movement.

Movement work itself introduces a new vocabulary. Words such as strong, spiky, curved, twisted, heavy, light, high, low, glide and flow are all used in this context.

Physical Education

The mathematical possibilities of the P.E. lesson become apparent in the use of apparatus. Children handle balls of different sizes made from different materials. Some bounce well, others hardly at all. From these experiences children become aware of the common property of these balls, the spatial property; they are all spheres. They handle hoops of varying size, made from different materials. These, too, have something in common: they are all the same shape — a circle. Getting in and out of hoops, bowling and spinning them, all this is valuable experience. If a hoop is broken or deformed it does not roll properly — only circles roll properly.

Using skipping ropes in a variety of ways helps to establish the notion of length.

e Bricks and constructional play
When there is a plentiful supply of bricks and boxes of all shapes and sizes, young children's imaginative play is enriched and much mathematical experience may be gained.

i Very large building
Once imaginative play has begun to develop in a young child there is a desire to play inside a house, a boat, an aeroplane, or a car of his own making. If nothing else is available, he will use a table or a chair for his make-believe indoors, or a corner of a shed or branches of trees outside. If space is available in a hall, corridor, porch or playground adjacent to a classroom, it is most desirable to provide a selection of large constructional apparatus.

Tea chests, fruit crates, boxes, barrels, an old table with legs sawn down, planks, boards, tyres, ropes, heavy cardboard rolls, and interesting and stimulating odds and ends such as an old steering wheel, a pair of handle-bars, straps, loudspeakers, handles, switches, etc.: all such things will give children an opportunity to build models on a large scale.

ii Building on floor or table
Even if there is not room to construct models large enough to play in, then smaller bricks can be provided, which do not take up so much storage space and which can be used on a fairly small patch of floor or even on table tops; but where possible these would be in addition to, or in conjunction with, the larger materials. The smaller bricks can also be made more interesting by providing smaller boxes, off-cuts of wood, hardboard, chipboard and polystyrene. They will be used for the building of harbours, airfields, docks, streets, forts, castles, farms, zoos, towns, markets, bus stations, railways, etc.

Road strips which children can lay out to form routes, tracks and circuits are of value as the problems they set are mathematical (fitting together shapes, angles, etc.).

iii Tiles
Tiles of all shapes and sizes may be provided for use, either separately or with bricks, so that the children make floors for their models, or distinguish various parts of their building, e.g. land from sea, one field from another, paths, roads.

Mathematical ideas involved in brick play
Children will have experience of sharing, counting, comparison and matching as they play, and occasionally the teacher may draw attention to this as she talks with them.

They are continually putting together three-dimensional shapes, finding which surfaces fit well together, which bricks make the best walls or seats, which surfaces balance best; they are frequently enclosing area in their play, and this together with discussion of the total area of the floor of the room, corridor or hall may help children to appreciate the adult concept of area. At first, perhaps, it might be referred to as 'floor space', as opposed to 'air space' (volume) taken up by an object.

The packing away of equipment will afford opportunity of making the best use of a limited space. Many teachers know how often young children fail to pack or stack equipment successfully; they will say that there is not enough room in a certain box or a certain place and with the method they have employed, there is not. But with practice and experience they learn how to use the available space efficiently, and how individual pieces will fit onto, beside, or inside each other.

Vocabulary

This describes space, shape, and size. The words big, bigger than, small, must be questioned and as soon as possible replaced by more meaningful statements about length, breadth, width, depth, height, space occupied or weight of objects under discussion. If a child is asked in what way a particular brick is bigger than another, he will have to think, to find words to describe his thoughts. If the necessary vocabulary is not within his experience, if meanings are confused or understanding not clear, then a chance is given for the child to learn and the teacher to discover more about the child's ability.

When describing the shape of bricks, boxes, boards, etc., only the simpler and more common names need be used with young children. However, it is within their power to understand that a solid shape has faces, because the word 'face' is already in their vocabulary, and that faces are bounded by edges; too often the word 'side' is used colloquially for both face and edge. Bricks with square faces may soon be given the name cubes, but others can continue to be referred to as rectangular, triangular or circular throughout the infants' school, unless a great interest in shape arises, when the children will force the pace and show their readiness for more knowledge. Before this, the words surface, flat, straight, round, curved, corner may be introduced, used and discussed.

It is evident that the activities described in this section prepare the children for more systematic work on space and for sophisticated use of standard measures of length, surface, volume and mass.

6 One-to-one correspondence and conservation of number

There is a long road between the first notion of a set and a real 'understanding' of number, which is acquired only gradually. Children comparatively early appreciate the 'twoness of two' and the 'threeness of three', but it should not be assumed that they can then automatically recognise or count up to 4, 5, 6, and so on (say to 10). It is, in fact, easy to be misled by the apparent ability of young children to count or even master simple operations. Do they, for example, really understand that the number of objects in a set does not alter when they are moved around? Or that numbers can be put in a definite order of magnitude 1, 2, 3, . . ., so that, for example, 3 is greater than 2, but 3 is less than 4?

Much practical experience is necessary before such ideas are firmly established. One-to-one correspondence, conservation of number, ordering and inclusion, are all important in the build-up of understanding of 'number'.

One-to-one correspondence

One of Piaget's experiments concerns matching. Children were presented with six egg-cups and a pile of eggs. They were asked to take some eggs so that there would be one for each egg-cup.

At the first stage of development, children were quite unable to do this. At the second stage, they were able to match one egg to each egg-cup and so arrive at the right total.

However, if the eggs were removed from the egg-cups and spread out so that the line of eggs extended beyond the line of egg-cups, then the children thought there were now more eggs than egg-cups.

This would occur even though only half a minute had elapsed since the child himself had matched the eggs to the egg-cups.

Experience of matching in a variety of ways in many different situations helps children to become aware of the number property of the sets they are matching.

Matching arises quite naturally at home on the basis of

'One for you and one for Mummy and one for me.'

The child matches one biscuit to each person. In home play he lays the table — one plate for each person, a blanket for each doll, and so on. It will arise naturally in school:
e.g. one pencil to each child, or one brush to each paint jar.

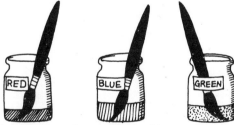

Again, model cars can be matched with garages : there might be only one garage into which each car fits ; alternatively the criterion might be for each car to be matched with the garage of the same colour. The banner shown on p. 7 is another example of one-to-one correspondence.

The vocabulary which children will develop in order to discuss their experiences will include such expressions as enough, more than, less than, one each, too many, not enough, too few.

The use of one-to-one correspondence in graph work
Graph work can give children valuable experience in matching, and will help the transition from the ability to match to the notion of number.

For example, one group of children were shown a box containing coloured cards. They each selected one card of their favourite colour. There was therefore a one-to-one correspondence between the children and the coloured cards. The cards were then stuck on paper in graph form.

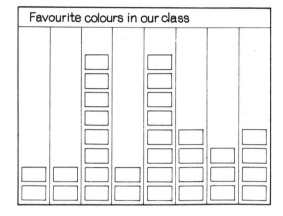

Favourite colours in our class

Much valuable discussion can arise from this kind of work. Matching is closely connected with the concept of invariance of number. As with the eggs and egg-cups, a child may readily agree that there is the same number of beads in these two rows :

But if the second lot is spread out, he may say that there are then more in the second row than in the first.

At a later stage, the child may 'see' that the number is the same in this case when there are 5 beads in each row, but not if there are, say, 12. Even counting does not always help : at a certain stage (at about 6) a child may well say there are 5 in each row but still assert that there are more in the second row ! There is a conflict between what he sees (apparently more in the second row) and what he knows, i.e. that the counters were in one-to-one correspondence before. His use of '5' may, in fact, be nothing more than saying a name. It is important that the teacher should know the stage which each child has reached and should provide much relevant experience, for example, the following:

Here is a bunch of flowers:

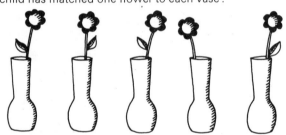

Here are some vases:

The child has matched one flower to each vase:

He accepts that there are as many flowers as vases.

Here he has put all the flowers in one vase, leaving four vases empty:

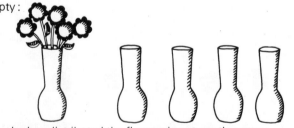

Here he has distributed the flowers in yet another way:

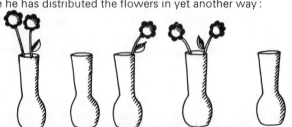

When the child is certain that however he arranged them there are always as many flowers as vases, the notion of invariance in this particular situation is established.

Again children can be asked to compare quantities and 'match up' one by one to see without counting if the collections have the same number of things in them.

'Have you as many pencils as Peter?'
'Have we enough sweets to give one to each child in the class?'
'Are there more objects in this pile than in that one?'

Such a comparison of miscellaneous collections helps to develop the idea that the number of objects in a pile is independent of their other properties (size, shape, colour, etc.).

Other types of correspondence
There are many instances both in and out of school when the correspondence is not one-to-one. This might be a useful topic for discussion with children who are already able to handle one-to-one correspondence with confidence, e.g.

We each have two eyes
                 ears
                 legs
                 feet
                 thumbs, etc.
We each wear two shoes
                 socks
                 gloves.

The children are becoming aware not only of the nature of one-to-one correspondence but also that in some instances a pair refers to two.

Examples of many-to-one correspondence are shown in the illustrations on pp. 13 and 25.

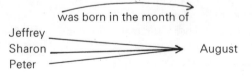

was born in the month of

Jeffrey
Sharon   August
Peter

Our   Birthdays

Jan. Feb. Mar. Apr. May June July Aug. Sep. Oct. Nov. Dec.

Experience of many-to-one correspondence can also be contrived in the classroom, for example:

It might be suggested to a child playing in the Home Corner that as it is such a cold day the dolls need three blankets each.

A bunch of flowers brought by a child might be distributed so that there are four flowers in each vase.

There are also, of course, 'many-to-many' correspondences, such as:

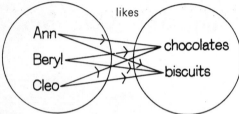

All these various types of correspondence will be encountered, but later the 'one-to-one' and 'many-to-one' will generally be more interesting mathematically.

7 Ordering and inclusion

Introduction

The last section was working towards the idea that a number stands for a class of things. The number 'two', for example, is an abstraction from all conceivable pairs: two apples, two bears, two carpets, two dreams, two eyes, two films, two greetings, two handshakes, two ideas, ... But this is not enough; another important property of numbers is that they can be compared with one another by being put in an order of magnitude: one, two, three, four, five, ... Three is greater than two; but also, three is less than four. At this time children will become familiar with the written symbols for numbers, the *numerals*, and will learn their order: 1, 2, 3, 4, 5, ... There are two ideas behind all this for children to grasp: ordering and inclusion. These should be developed in parallel.

Ordering

The ordering of numbers one, two, three, four, . . . is quite a sophisticated idea, and we shall first go back to the more primitive notions of 'order'. Even the relations *is greater than, is taller than,*

is thinner than are all more complicated for a child to sort out than the simple idea of being lined up in some way. The simplest form of ordering is that of the queue, the child seeing that he is in front of John and Jane but behind Jill and Kevin as he lines up for dinner. Children can acquire further experience by reproducing a line of shapes.

Of course a box containing plenty of duplicates of these (and perhaps others) has to be provided. As usual, children learn in the first instance by doing, by actually handling the shape, and again they can cope progressively with a greater number. The child should first be asked to make a straight copy, starting, say, from the left.

Given row

He may see, for example, that ■ is placed next door to ▲ and to the right of it. He will also begin to appreciate that ordering is transitive, e.g.

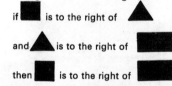

Instructions can be given such as 'Show me all the shapes which are to the right of ▬ '.

The next stage is to see whether the child can copy, but with the order reversed:

If a child can complete this task, he has managed to isolate and really understand the primitive notion of ordering.

After this, a relationship can be imposed, such as *is taller than*. For example, a set of trees is to be arranged in a definite order of height.

The differences in height should be irregular and small enough to make the children think — and put the trees they want to compare side by side. First they will actually do the ordering and only later be able to describe their method. As a check of understanding, the teacher may ask, 'Show me all the trees taller than this one'. Of course experiences should be varied and include trees, houses, sticks, the children themselves, etc.

The illustrations on pp. 28 and 29 show early experiences of ordering, putting things in order of size. The family graph shows the arrangement of a family in order of size, beginning with the smallest member. The three bears and their belongings are placed in order of size beginning with the largest.

For many years children have played with nesting boxes. This piece of equipment consists of hollow cuboids of graduated size with one face missing. It is essential to fit the boxes inside each other in the right order or you will find that you have a box or boxes over.

A set of tin lids or buttons of graduated size is a more flexible piece of equipment.

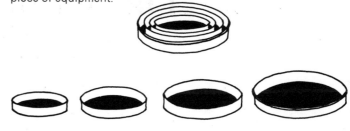

Not only can these be placed on top of each other in size order beginning with the largest, but they can be arranged in rows in many directions, as the arrows show.

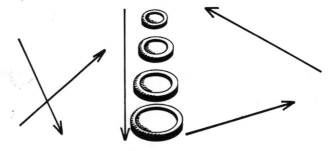

After a period of free play with these materials, children might be asked to see in how many different ways they can arrange the lids, remembering to keep them in size order.

In one school the Home Corner was equipped with a series of graduated dolls, each fully dressed and with its own bed and bed-clothes. This provided the children with many opportunities of matching and ordering. They could not only match the right clothes to the doll, and bedding to the bed, but experiment in arranging dolls, clothes, beds and bedding in size order.

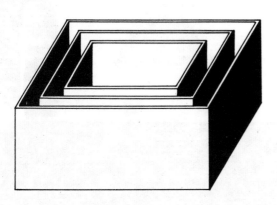

nesting boxes

The Family Graph.

Father is bigger than mother

Mother is bigger than brother

Brother is bigger than sister

Sister is bigger than baby

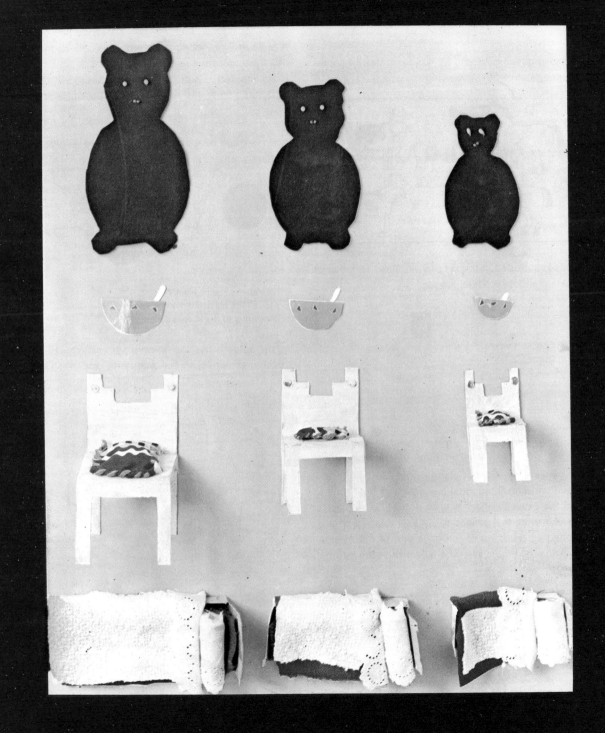

Inclusion

The idea that, for example, 4< 7 (read as '4 is less than 7') comes also from experiences such as the following:

The set of 4 horses is included in the set of 7 animals. The idea of inclusion fascinates children at a later stage:

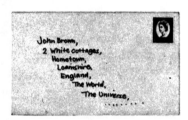

It has indeed already been built into earlier sorting activities. When children sort out buttons from a sorting box they are in fact picking out objects which have been included in the whole collection. But usually they do not think about this. They are concerned only with finding things that are alike and distinguishing them from all the other things. They do not relate the things they are picking out with the collection as a whole. Two new thoughts are needed: a selection of things is **part** of the original collection; the **number** of things selected is less than the number in the whole set.

The idea of inclusion, or of the part being contained in the whole, is not so 'obvious' as may appear to us as adults.

2 black and 10 white buttons

A child of 6 or 7 confronted with this collection may well say that there are more white buttons than there are buttons – he cannot yet compare the part (the white buttons) with the whole (all the buttons) and so instead compares the white ones with the black ones.

Again a good deal of experience should be given, with all sorts of materials, animals, flowers, fruits, ...

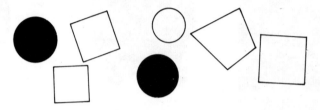

Are all the circles black?
Are all the black shapes circles?
Are some of the shapes squares?

Again, actually making 'Venn diagrams' (pp. 14, 15) by enclosing the shapes with string or wire helps understanding.

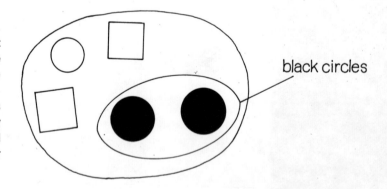

black circles

These experiences of inclusion are, of course, leading further than comparison of numbers (4< 7, etc.). Knowing the difference between 'all' and 'some' is a big step towards being able to think logically.

Another idea to be acquired at about the same time is the notion of a complement. If we pick out some elements of a set as a sub-set, then the remaining elements form the complement of this sub-set. For example, if the boys are selected from the class, the complement will consist of the girls. This eventually leads back to number:

2 black and 10 white buttons

The set of 4 horses is included in the set of 7 animals; its complement is the set of 3 cows.

'4 animals and 3 animals; altogether 7 animals'

It is, in fact, possible now to bring the threads together and look at the whole question of 'understanding number'.

8 Pictorial representation
Stages of development

It is very important that the teacher should be aware of the various stages of presentation of a new mathematical idea if the children are to grow to understand it. The correct moment for taking the child into the next stage will be decided by the observant teacher. It is impossible to lay down any defined programme for a child of any given age.

An outline of the main stages in the development of pictorial representation is given below, though intermediate stages may well arise with individual children.

Stage 1

In the first instance it might be best to keep to the simplest form of one-to-one correspondence, i.e. one object (brick, milk bottle, bead, etc.) for each child. Children will begin to accept that if everyone is holding a bead, there must be the same number of beads, or as many beads, as children.

This equality, however, is of less significance in the early stages than the idea of inequality.

Greater than, less than, more than, fewer than, is the kind of vocabulary that children will acquire and use in a meaningful way. Our aim at this stage is to clarify the use of the word *big*, and in the context of pre-counting activities help the children towards the real understanding of *more than* and *less than*.

Three ways of comparing the number of boys and girls in our class

1 Comparison of two rows of bricks, lino tiles or milk bottles. Each child places his own object in position, to represent himself.

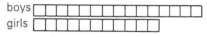

2 Pieces of dowel rod or large knitting needles. Each child places a washer or curtain ring on the appropriate rod.

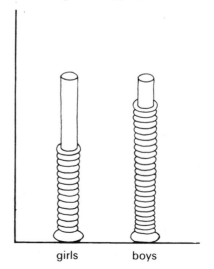

girls   boys

3 Each child puts his own bead on the appropriate string. When complete these strings are suspended and compared.

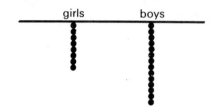

At this stage two things are important:

1 that there is one object for every child involved in the work, i.e. one-to-one correspondence.

2 that comparison is only made between *two* rows or columns, this being the necessary first step in building more complicated relationships.

Progress made by the children will be largely determined by the amount of time devoted to discussion of the data and their representation.

Further suggestions
Children who go home alone.
Children who are met by mother.
Children who have brothers and sisters in school.
Children who have no brothers or sisters in school.

Suitable materials can be found in any environment. The one essential property is that the things used should be the same size, e.g. a set of bottle tops.

Stage 2
a An increase in the number of data, moving from the comparison of two columns to the comparison of several columns.
b Transition to some more permanent form of recording, e.g. the 'matchbox' graph.

Our birthdays
(See p. 25)

i Each child has a matchbox, covers it with plain paper, and writes his name on it. The matchboxes are then stuck in the appropriate column. Much discussion will arise from this work.

ii

| January |
| February |
| March |
| April |
| May |
| June |
| July |
| August |
| September |
| October |
| November |
| December |

Each child makes a drawing of himself on a suitably sized piece of paper, cuts it out and sticks it in the appropriate row.

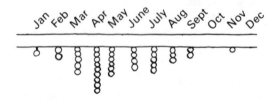

Here, beads or interlocking curtain rings are suspended from the appropriate hook.

At this level, after a great deal of discussion, children may be capable of formulating and considering a real problem, e.g. 'Are there always more people born in April than in any other month?'

How could we find out? We might collect further information, e.g. teachers' birthdays; mothers' birthdays; fathers' birthdays; the birthdays of the children in the class next door.

Other suggestions for this stage of graph work
The colour of the clothes the children are wearing.
The site of their homes.

Stage 3
As Stage 2, but representation on paper by pictures, leading eventually to squares which are stuck on, e.g.
(7 model buses)→(7 pictures of a bus)→(7 'squares', one for each bus).

Introducing block charts
Suggested topic: Pets.

Not every child in the class will have a pet and some children will have more than one. The number of objects represented on the chart will be equal to the number of pets owned.

At this stage we are making the transition from the pictorial chart to the block chart, and this is illustrated below:

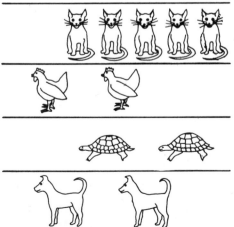

Figure 1

In a particular project the children were asked to make drawings of their pets. They then cut out the drawings and stuck them on paper. No guidance was given. It can be seen that in this form, i.e. the haphazard sticking on of pictures, nothing emerges clearly. This situation can lead to much profitable discussion; the children readily agreed that it would be better if they had a proper starting place. This kind of discovery will help towards the eventual understanding of an 'axis'.

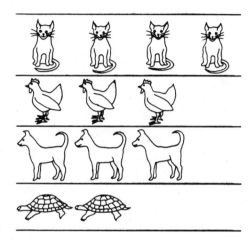

Figure 2

Now we can see quite clearly that there are more cats than dogs, and more birds than tortoises. If children are allowed to encounter difficulties in this way and suggest possible solutions themselves, much progress will be made.

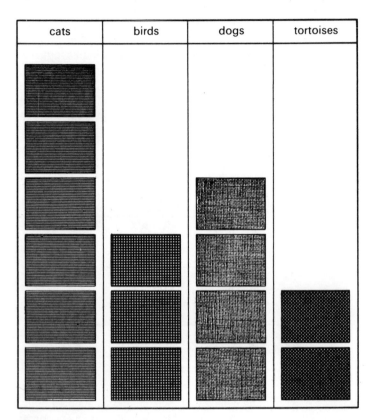

| cats | birds | dogs | tortoises |

Figure 3

In Fig. 3 the children used squares of coloured paper and stuck them in columns on a chart prepared by the teacher. This 'sticking on' of squares is a progression from sticking on matchboxes or pictures. It shows the transition stage from representation by three-dimensional objects to the use of a block chart.

Before counting is established, such a block chart will enable the children to make comparisons without finding the number of animals in each set. But the way is now open for Stage 4 to develop when squares can be coloured on squared paper and the *numbers* in each category can be shown.

Part III
Number begins

1 Towards number

With the various experiences so far described, children will gradually come to appreciate 'number' in its dual role:

a one, two, three, four, . . . ('cardinal').

b first, second, third, fourth, . . . ('ordinal').

Isolated numbers like one, two or seven often refer to an actual amount without reference to any order or comparison with other numbers. These cardinal numbers will gradually become familiar by acquaintance with four aeroplanes, five horses, six matchboxes, etc. and, just as important, four, five, six, . . . miscellaneous objects in a heap. To find the number of objects in a collection, it is generally necessary to count, that is, to match the objects in turn against the numbers of the standard set one, two, three, ... Learning to count comes gradually. At first children may well count 'one, two, three, four, . . .' getting quite out of step with the objects concerned, or perhaps getting lost and counting some objects more than once. It is not sufficiently recognised that there is a great gulf between the ability to recite the number words in sequence and the ability to match the saying of the word to the moving of the object. This is, after all, what we are asking children to do when we say 'Show me five pencils'. It is impossible to teach a child this skill; he will gain it gradually through much experiment.

Provision for counting experience

Realising that they are allowed to put the 'counted' objects on one side helps children to do the task correctly; sometimes it is helpful to provide counters or buttons of different colours, or a collection of quite different-looking objects, making it easier to remember which have been accounted for. Some children will acquire the skill of counting with a minimum of difficulty. Their level of development will become apparent through their conversation, and the comments they make about their various activities.

For example:

Referring to preliminary work concerning the comparison of two rows or columns, the child who can not only comment 'There are more boys than girls in our class today', but also 'There are five more boys than girls in our class today', is already acquiring the skill of counting. Others will not find it so easy. They might be able to say that there were more boys than girls, but will be unable accurately to answer the question 'How many more?'.

In day-to-day work in the classroom there are many opportunities for real counting experience. During the discussion at the beginning of the session a teacher might say:

> Four children may use the clay today.
> Five may play in the Home Corner.
> Only two at the water tray, please.
> Not more than three at the woodwork bench.

Numerals

Number symbols, i.e. numerals, are all around us and children will gradually come to associate them correctly with the numbers they have learned orally. This point is well made in the following extract from the Mathematical Association's *The Teaching of Mathematics in Primary Schools*. (This report, written in 1955, was well in advance of its time. A second, follow-up report (1970) is also well worth reading.) 'The figures which represent numbers are familiar to children before they come to school; they see them on the price tickets in shops, on buses and on hoardings; some of the figures will be known and named. In schools, pictures illustrating rhymes or stories will sometimes include figures; the classroom clock and the order for so many bottles of milk will also show figures which the children will talk about. As oral counting proceeds, some of the activities will demand the labelling of objects with the symbol of their place in the sequence, as for example the numbering of tickets and chairs for an audience. The number of goods in stock in the classroom shop will be pasted on the containers, price tickets will be written on goods for sale. In these ways the learning of written number form grows with its meaning. . . .'

Much experience should occur naturally in reading and writing the numbers which arise in daily activities, so that there will be less need for formal matching apparatus.

Class or group booklets

A class or group booklet can be helpful, e.g.

'A book about four.'

On each page there is a child's drawing and a caption, written by either the child or the teacher, e.g.

> A table has four legs.
> A car has 4 wheels.
> My daddy's car has four doors.
> We have 4 cats at home.
> I live at number 4.
> Billy is about 4 feet high.

This particular example illustrates how a child can begin to appreciate that

> four and 4

are sometimes interchangeable.

Checking on the fiveness of five

The following sequence is intended to help the teacher to assess just how far Jane has got in her understanding of five.

i Jane is asked to count out five sweets from a pile. If she removes from the pile any number of sweets either greater or less than five then as yet she is unable to count. This is not a mistake which can be corrected. She has simply not arrived yet at that level of development and needs a lot more experience of the kind already described.

ii If Jane accurately counts out five sweets, then the teacher might scatter them over the table and ask 'How many sweets have I got?'.

If Jane says 'Why five, of course' and really considers it a silly question, then she has established conservation of five. She knows that however you arrange the sweets there are still five.

However, if in reply to the question 'How many sweets have I got?' Jane repeats the process and counts the sweets again, then the invariance of five as yet eludes her.

iii Further verification of conservation can be obtained by grouping five in different ways, and asking 'Which lot of sweets would you rather have?'.

this

or this?

Ordinal numbers

Many children are helped at home by their mothers to acquire the ability to say number words in sequence. When mother and child climb a short flight of stairs, counting as they go, the mother says as her foot touches each stair, 'one . . . two . . . three', etc. The child may be joining in with her. What are they really doing? They are giving a name to each stair. It will be a long time before the child will be able to tell you that stair three comes before stair four and after stair two.

We should be more accurate if, when we climb stairs with children, we say 'first . . . second . . . third', etc., to emphasise that we are now interested in the order.

Number ladders

When children use the number ladder they will see that it requires more effort to climb 5 stairs than 4, that you get higher by climbing 7 instead of 3, and so on; they will realise that they have greater spending power if they have 6p instead of 4p.

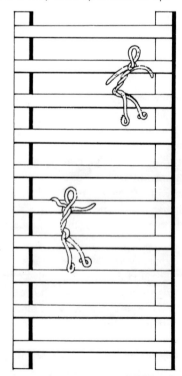

All these experiences lead to the idea of an ordering relation on the sequence of 'counting numbers', 1, 2, 3, 4, 5, . . . Given any subset, say $\{7, 4, 92, 17, 43\}$, we can put these numbers in a definite order: 4, 7, 17, 43, 92; in this arrangement each number is less than the ones that follow it.

For a child beginning to understand number relationships, a number ladder is a useful piece of equipment. The most profitable uses of the ladder will be those games and activities suggested by the children, but here are some suggestions:

a Two children, each with a pipe-cleaner doll, are playing together with the ladder. After some free play introduce a die. Each child throws, then moves his doll-man up the ladder, the number of rungs climbed being equal to the number of dots on the die. A possible recording:

> Jane threw 3 on the die.
> Peter threw 5 on the die.
> Peter's man is higher up the ladder.
> $5 > 3$.

b The two children throw again. Jane's man climbs up 5 rungs. Peter's man climbs up 2 rungs. 'How many more rungs would Peter's man have to climb up in order to join Jane's man?'

> Jane threw 5 on the die.
> Peter threw 2 on the die.
> Peter's man is lower down the ladder.
> $5 > 2$.
> Jane's man would have to climb down 3 rungs to be with Peter's man.

Not every try needs recording in this way. The examples given indicate the way in which children should be encouraged to talk and think about the situation.

Number-strips

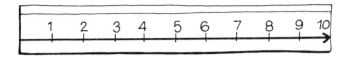

It is only possible to move in two ways on a number ladder, either up or down.

A number-strip is a much more flexible tool, in that it can be used in many different directions.

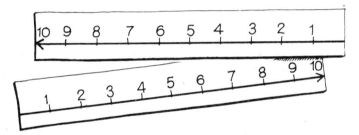

If strips are made from wood or thick card, children will be able to handle them easily and place them in different directions.

Some suggestions concerning work with number-strips

A number-strip could be chalked on the playground, the child actually jumping along it.

Toy men could be used to move along the strip. Finally, the strip alone will be sufficient.

Finding out about numbers

Here are some further suggestions for helping children to find out about numbers.

Ask the child to put out several heaps of five pebbles. He will probably arrange his collection of five quite haphazardly, possibly something like this:

Ask him to leave one lot untouched, and to arrange the others in as many different ways as he can, to see what he can find out about 5.

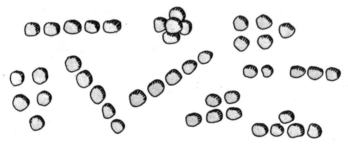

things I can do with a collection of 5 pebbles.

Recording

There will come a time when it will be appropriate for children to start recording their work with numbers. In all probability it will be for many children rather later in their school lives than was the former practice. Our increased knowledge of child development and the problems of individual differences makes it possible to form more objective judgements as to when this suggestion of recording is appropriate.

Initially children will record in simple graph form or in words. Gradually they will come to realise that 4 is but a useful shorthand for four, and the number symbols or numerals will be meaningful.

When children have some sense of both the ordinal and cardinal aspects of number, we would do well to encourage them to consider number relationships in words, e.g.

seven is more than six,
five is less than eight.

This will be a refinement of

seven is bigger than six,
five is smaller than eight.

Children will sooner or later see that it is much quicker to write

$7 > 6,$
$5 < 8.$

Before attempting this step forward the teacher should be sure that the child understands number, say to ten, in both ordinal and cardinal aspects and that he is completely familiar with the numerals to ten and understands that they are useful shorthand symbols for the words.

The symbol for *is greater than* is $>$, e.g. $7 > 5$.
The symbol for *is less than* is $<$, e.g. $3 < 5$.

It is best to use the symbols only to compare two numbers. They should not be used as an abbreviation in the middle of a sentence, such as 'My pocket money $>$ yours'.

Sheila   Arthur   7-8   1A2

Block Graph to Show Our Team Point's

Point's

| Team's | Red | Blue | Green | Yellow |

Sheila   Arthur
1. Red and Blue had 1 less than Green.
2. Yellow had the most Point's.
3. Yellow had 3 more than Green.
4. Red and Blue made a draw.
5. Green had 1 more than Blue and Red.
6. Yellow had 8 team Point's.
7. Green had 5 Point's.
8. Blue had 4 Point's.
9. Red had 4 Point's.

Children have usually now reached another stage in making graphs and can use squared paper with squares coloured in and numbers shown.

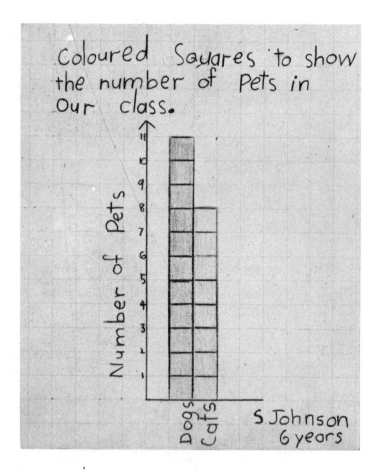

Coloured Squares to show the number of Pets in Our class.

Number of Pets

Dogs
Cats

S. Johnson
6 years

The children in our class have 11 dogs and 8 cats. There are 11 squares in The dog row and only 8 squares in the cat row. If we count the squares we can see that 11 > 8 and 8 < 11. There are 3 more dogs than cats. If we count up all the squares there are 19 Pets because 11 + 8 = 19. 19 is nine 2's and 1 over. 19 is an odd number. There are 10 children who have dogs because Craig has 2 dogs Called Bruce and Susan.

There are 5 children who have cats, because Janet lives at a farm and they have 4 cats. They have a dog Too. They have 4 + 1 = 5 Pets. Only Janet had both kinds of Pets.

2 Operations and the use of symbols

Equality

In mathematics the term 'equality' infers a relationship that is unambiguous and is represented by the symbol '='. This symbol is quite familiar, though it is often misused or abused.

We shall use the symbol '=' at present only to denote 'represents the same number as'.

Children need many counting experiences.

Peter takes three nuts from a bowl, then another two. The teacher asks 'How many have you got now?' 'Five,' says Peter proudly.

The problem of recording experiences now arises. Hitherto a combination of practical experiences and discussion has been the first stage in the development of the notion of number. The second stage is entered upon when Peter can record his experience using the written word, e.g.

I had 3 nuts, then I took 2 more, so now I have 5.

The writing involved can be burdensome, and so we tend to introduce a shorthand version in the form of a mathematical statement:

$3+2=5.$

This statement deals with pure numbers, that is with abstractions. But Peter was concerned with counting out nuts. He had 3 and then 2 more. He put them together, counted them and found that altogether he now had 5 nuts. This indicated to him that having 3 and 2 he had altogether 5. '3 and 2 *is equal to* 5' would be misleading: he did not have another 5 nuts to which the 2 and 3 were equal, but just the original nuts.

3 and 2, altogether 5

Such statements as

my ribbon = 8 inches,
my pink mouse = 3 ounces,

are a serious abuse of the symbol of mathematical equality.

What Jane means is:

'I measured my ribbon and it is about 8 inches long.
My pink mouse weighs about 3 ounces.'

The symbol of equality is entirely inappropriate here. A special note on the implications of the 'equals sign' is given on p. 53.

Addition

Addition can be defined as an *operation*, one number being added to another number, resulting in a third number. In a cookery recipe you are instructed to add the sugar to the existing mixture. This is a physical operation. You actually add the sugar by pouring it into the mixing bowl.

Addition of numbers, whilst still being an operation, is not physical but mental. When we consider the numbers '3' and '2' and the operation 'add' applied to them, we arrive at '5'. This is an abstract operation performed in the mind and is indicated by the symbol '+', mathematically translatable as *plus*.

Addition is, in fact, defined in terms of cardinal numbers of sets which have no common elements.

In the diagram, the number of elements in the set of thin fish is 4 and the number in the set of fat fish is 3.

The *union* of two sets consists of the set of all elements which belong to at least one of them. Here the union is a set of 7 fish (4 of which are thin and 3 fat). Since our original sets had no elements in common the cardinal number (namely 7) of their union set is the result of adding their cardinal numbers (which are 4 and 3 respectively).

A story of seven fish

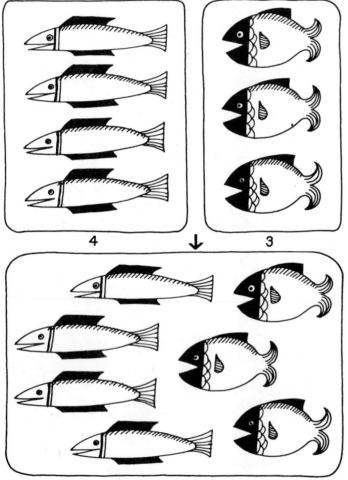

Mapping

If we accept that the traditional symbols '+', '−', '=' are inappropriate for children still largely concerned with concrete objects in their experiments with, and experience of, numbers, we must search for another way of recording which will bridge the gap between words and equations.

1 **Words:** I had 3 nuts, then I took 2 more, so now I have 5.
2 **Equation:** $3 + 2 = 5$.

A way to bridge this gap is to use the idea of *mapping*.

In the example on p. 43 each child in the class mapped his or her own name onto the month in which he or she was born.

The word mapping and the use of an arrow were easily accepted by the children who explained it in these words: 'It tells you where to go'.

In this next example the children started with any number in the first set, performed an operation on that number, i.e. added 1, and so were able to map it onto the appropriate number in the second set.

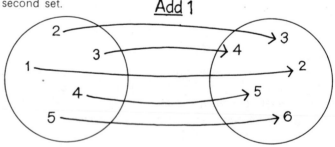

An alternative representation might be:

Add 1

3 ⟶ 4
1 ⟶ 2
4 ⟶ 5
2 ⟶ 3
5 ⟶ 6

Birthdays

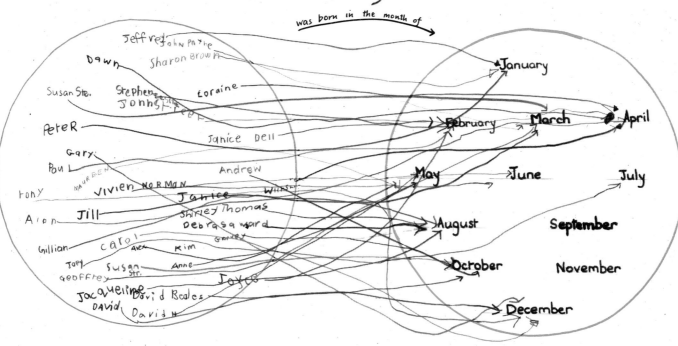

was born in the month of ⟶

Jeffrey John Paine
Dawn Sharon Brown
Susan Ste. Stephen Loraine
John H. Free
Peter
Janice Dell
Gary
Paul Andrew
Tony Maureen Vivien Norman
Alan Jill Janice Winst
Shirley Thomas
Debra Saward
Gillian Carol Garry
Alex Kim
Joey Susan Anne
Geoffrey Str.
Jacqueline Joyce
David David Beales
David H.

January
February March April
May June July
August September
October November
December

The set of all the children in the class.   The set of all the months of the year

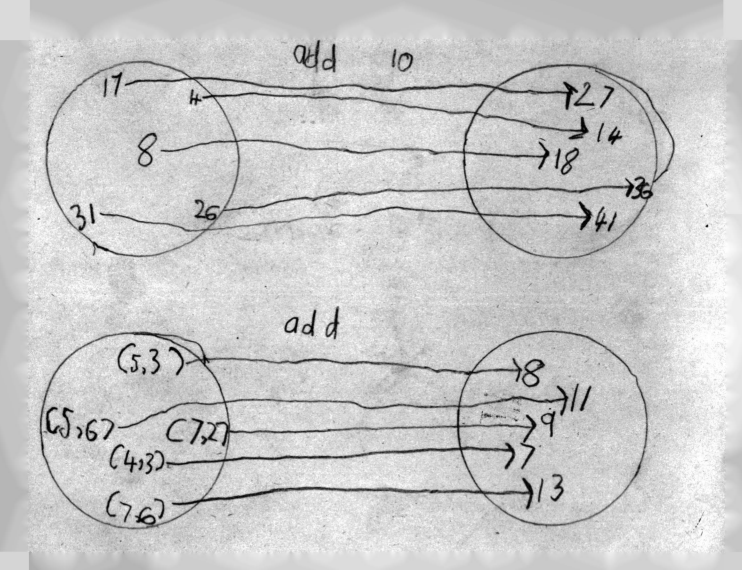

Earlier in this book (see p. 11) we considered the relation 'placed in water, will' and saw that this can be shown as a mapping, for by slightly altering diagram (c) on p. 11 we obtain the diagram below. Here the arrow tells us 'where to go'. If more than one arrow should leave an element of the first set, then we should be in doubt about 'where to go'. As we shall see, many such relations do exist but we do not call such relations *mappings*.

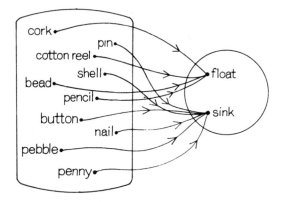

The test for a mapping is that one and not more than one arrow should leave elements of the first set. The above mapping is 'many-to-one', as many arrows may arrive at either 'float' or 'sink' but one only may leave 'cork', 'pencil', etc. (See also pp. 23-26.)

If it also happens that no element of the second set is at the head of more than one arrow, then we say that the mapping is 'one-to-one'.

Examples : diagrams showing the colour of coat peg used by various children :

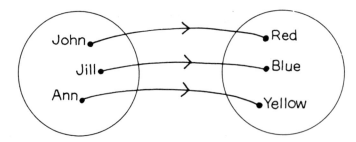

This is a one-to-one mapping.

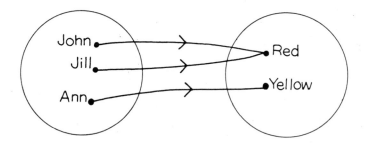

This is a many-to-one mapping.

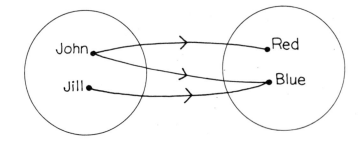

This is not a mapping at all, since John seems to be using both the red and the blue coat pegs. Of course this does not mean that such a thing could not happen — it is just a question of how mathematicians define the word 'mapping'.

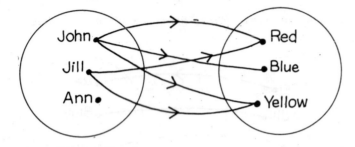

This again is a possible situation, but not a 'mapping'. Ann has no peg at all and John and Jill each use more than one.

The idea of mapping is an important one in mathematics. It makes life less complicated when the elements of two sets are related in such a way that, given a member of the first set, you know the corresponding member of the second.

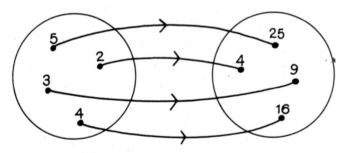

For example, here the elements in the first set are mapped onto their squares.

Addition (continued)

The ways of recording addition on p. 42 are examples of mapping. Below is another representation, the instruction being 'add the two numbers forming the ordered pair'.

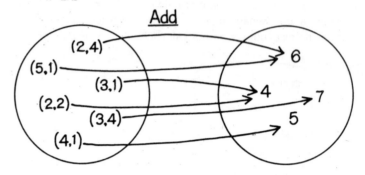

For example, the arrow leading from (2, 4) to 6 means 'Start with the numbers 2 and 4, add them together and show the result (namely 6)'. This has been found a clear way for young children to record their findings; it is also akin to the language of the computer. The mapping could be recorded in this way:

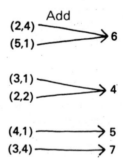

When children can transfer information and display it in a clearer way without any assistance from the teacher, it will be evident that they are beginning to perceive relationships.

In this instance the child will have seen that (2,4) and (5,1) both map onto 6 under addition.

Number relations

Teachers have always been aware of the significance of number relationships. We now know that for these to be meaningful and interrelated, children must be allowed to discover the relationships for themselves. The teacher's task is to contrive such situations. In solving the problems that arise, children will make these discoveries, as the following example illustrates.

Materials

A bag of pebbles (to be used if necessary).
A set of ordered pairs of numbers, written as under:

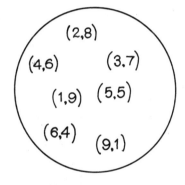

Problem: Are there any pairs missing from this set?
Children will approach this problem in many different ways. One possible way is illustrated:

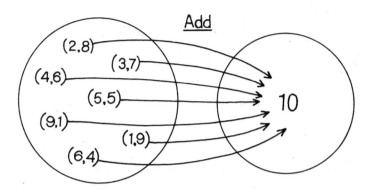

They all map onto 10.

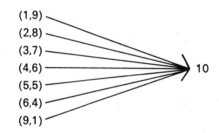

A child might possibly record as follows:

'When I tried to put these pairs in order I found that some pairs were missing. The first numbers of each pair go like this: 1, 2, 3, 4, 5, 6, 9, so I think 7 and 8 are missing. The second numbers of each pair go like this: 9, 8, 7, 6, 5, 4, 1, so I think 3 and 2 are missing. All the pairs add to 10 so the missing pairs must be (7,3) and (8,2).'

Here a child was finding out about 10. In order to do so it was necessary that he should be able to:

i understand the cardinal aspect of number.
(This enabled him to see, after a few preliminary experiments, that his problem concerned the number 10.)

ii understand the ordinal aspect of number.
(This enabled him to see a possible pattern in the arrangement of the pairs. He saw that the first numbers of the pairs were 1, 2, 3, 4, 5, 6, 9, and knew that 7 and 8 were missing.)

Pre-subtraction experience

'Subtraction' has been too often a mysterious process, introduced too early and unmeaningfully. Much of the trouble is concerned with premature introduction of the 'minus sign' and loose talk about 'taking away'.

The first approach to 'subtraction' concerns the comparison between two rows or columns, one of which is greater than the other (cf. p. 33, pets in our class).

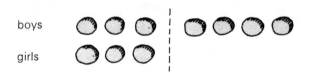

boys

girls

If the top row indicates the number of boys in a set of children and the bottom row the number of girls, then young children will immediately be able to determine that there are more boys than girls. In order to answer the question 'How many more?' most children will use the technique of matching (one-to-one correspondence) as far as possible, and then count the remaining boys, arriving at the solution, 'There are 4 more boys than girls'. This illustrates the aspect of subtraction normally referred to as 'the difference between'.

From such experience there develops the idea of complementary addition (counting on).

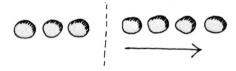

In this instance, the child 'counts on' from 3. These ways of leading up to 'subtraction' can be illuminated by using the language of sets. Suppose in a certain set of children some stay to school dinner ('stayers') and others go home ('goers') as follows:

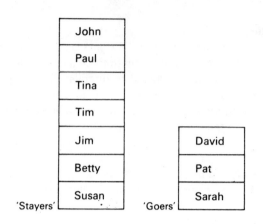

The total is made up of the 'stayers' and the 'goers'.

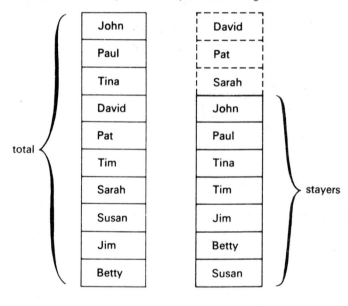

If the total number is known and also the number of the 'stayers', then the number of 'goers' can be found by counting on. When a set is partitioned into two sub-sets each of these is the complement of the other, as, for example:

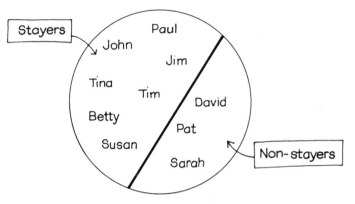

The set of 'non-stayers' is the complement of the set of 'stayers': together they form the total set of children.

Can mapping help?
Counting backwards:
10→ 9→ 8→ 7→ 6→ 5→ 4→ 3→ 2→ 1

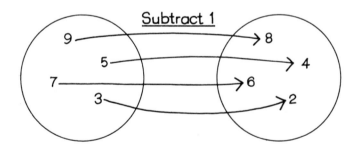

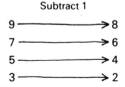

Can we use ordered pairs?
The operation here is 'take the second number from the first'. 'Subtraction' has not yet been formally defined. The problem, as suggested above, is really 'What must be added to the second number to give the first?'

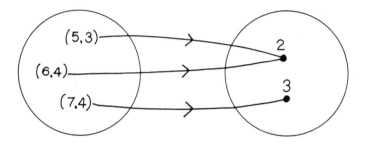

The above diagram shows a mapping of the three ordered pairs in the first set onto the corresponding numbers in the second set, e.g. (5,3) is mapped onto 2. We can say that 2 is the image of (5,3) under the mapping. If we put (3,5)

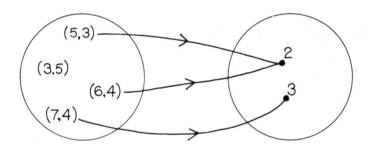

into the set of ordered pairs, we no longer have a mapping, since we cannot find an image for (3,5). In other words 'take 5 from 3' is a process not defined in the set of numbers with which we are dealing. We have, in fact, up to now been concerned with the set of counting numbers (or, as they are sometimes called, 'natural' numbers), {1, 2, 3, 4, 5, . . . }. Later the children will encounter other sets of numbers in which, for example, 'negative 2' will be defined.

Addition. Does order matter?

Children who are familiar with the use of the ordered pair will be able to experiment on their own and discover for themselves that

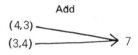

Add
(4,3)
(3,4) ⟶ 7

With encouragement they will go on to discover for themselves that in every case of addition, one can reverse the order of the pairs and obtain the same result. They will be discovering for themselves the principle of *commutativity*:

Four plus three gives the same number as three plus four.

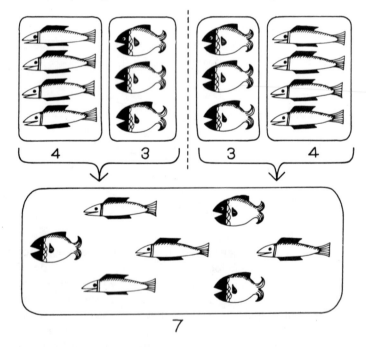

The idea of commutativity is an important one and not just confined to the addition of numbers. For instance, multiplication of two numbers is commutative, e.g. $7\times8=8\times7$. This simply means that both 7×8 and 8×7 represent the number 56; the

order does not matter. At a later stage, children will discover that $7-5$ is not the same as $5-7$, so subtraction is non-commutative: the order does matter. Children sometimes enjoy discussing whether the order matters or not in various situations, e.g.

> I put on my socks and then my shoes.

Does this have the same effect as

> I put on my shoes and then my socks?

Towards multiplication

In this section we trace the underlying ideas of multiplication.

Of course preliminary experience is desirable, for example with the equal rows in patty tins.

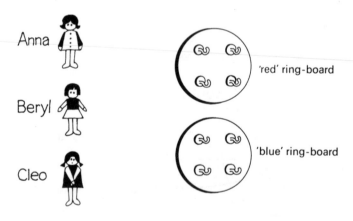

Anna

Beryl

Cleo

'red' ring-board

'blue' ring-board

Three children are playing with two ring-boards. A 'turn' at the game consists of throwing a ring and hoping to make a score by landing it on one of the hooks on the boards.

Each child has one turn with each board. How many turns are there altogether?

These could be listed as ordered pairs:

(Anna, red)   (Beryl, blue)
(Anna, blue)   (Cleo, red)
(Beryl, red)   (Cleo, blue)

Now, by counting the number of ordered pairs, the total of six turns is reached. Essentially the multiplication of 3 and 2 consists of this process. Another way of going about the problem would be to match Anna and 'red', etc., like this:

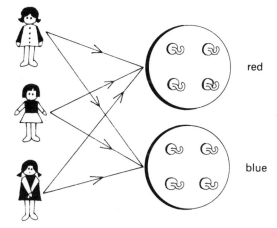

Counting the number of lines joining members of the set of three girls to the members of the set of two ring-boards again gives as the product the number 6.

A particular model of multiplication is afforded by the traditional lines of soldiers (four rows of three soldiers or three columns of four soldiers).

In both the examples we have seen, children throwing rings and soldiers on parade, two distinct sets are involved. First, it was the girls and the ring-boards, e.g. Anna's turn with the red board. Next, the soldiers can be identified by means of their row and column, e.g. the man in the second row and third column. Much later,

X	1	2	3	4
1	1	2	3	4
2	2	4	6	8

6 is the product of 2 (*second* row) and 3 (*third* column). In fact 6 is in the second row and the third column.

All this may suggest the need for some preliminary experience such as the following:

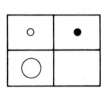

key	
small white counter	small black counter
large white counter	?

i A heap of small/large, black/white counters is provided. What type of counter 'belongs' in the last square?

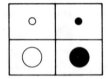

(A large, black one, being in the 'large' row and the 'black' column).

ii Gradual build-up of this idea, e.g.

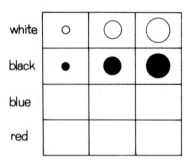

iii

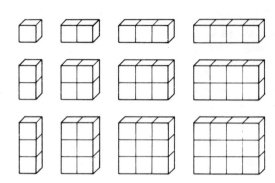

Build-up of patterns: for example, the above. This pattern represents piles of cubical bricks. The pile in the third row and second column contains six bricks; it is '3 high', because that is the property of all the piles in the third row, and '2 long' because that is the property of all the piles in the second column.

3 Summary

The following is a reminder of some of the mathematical notions introduced so far.

a Sets

A collection of objects is called a *set* if it is clear that any given one of the objects really does belong to the collection.

b Relations

A 'relation' is given by listing ordered pairs: the relationship exists between each first member and the corresponding second member.

The relation may be between members of the same set, e.g. for the numbers 1, 2, 3, 4 and the relation $>$, we have

(4,3)
(4,2)
(4,1)
(3,2)
(3,1)
(2,1)

In each pair the first number is greater than the second: $4 > 3$, $2 > 1$. This particular relation is an 'ordering relation'.

Or the relation may be between members of different sets, e.g. (p.6).

(Peter, bat)
(Jane, ball)

the relation being *has a*.

c   Partitioning of a set
(p. 12) A partition consists of dividing a set into 'sub-sets' such that each sub-set contains at least one element and each element belongs to just one sub-set.

d   One-to-one correspondence, see for example p. 24, where there is one flower for each vase, and each vase has just one flower.

e   The idea of **mapping** seems to help in early recording, before the familiar symbols $+$, $-$, $\times$, $\div$ are meaningful. A mapping from one set to another is a correspondence between elements such that just one element in the second set corresponds to each element in the first (cf. p. 45).

An 'element' of the first set might, for example, be an ordered pair, while the rule determining its image in the second set might be 'add', see p. 46.

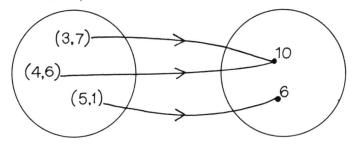

As by now will be evident, the notion of a *set* is fundamental in mathematics. At the lowest level, the mere fact that there are sets of numbers, sets of points, sets of solutions of equations, and so on, gives a link between topics previously thought of as quite distinct and isolated. Later, emphasis on the particular set being considered in a particular problem will avoid howlers like '$10\frac{1}{2}$ men are required for the job'.

The mapping of elements of one set onto those of another is a way of looking at the idea of a *function*, which is at the heart of later mathematics. The speed of a rocket, for example, depends on the time elapsed after take-off. Given the time, it is possible to predict or plot the corresponding speed unambiguously, so that there is a mapping 'from the time to the speed'.

This is, of course, only a glimmering of the development of mathematics. But it is remarkable how closely related are the widely used inventions of 20th century mathematicians and the work for children described in this book.

4   A note on relations and the equals sign *
Quite a number of different relations have been discussed, e.g.

is taller than,
belongs to,
has the same colour as.

From these it is clear that where a relation exists, it is between the members of a pair and, further, that the members of the pair are ordered. Thus, 'Jane is taller than John' applies to the members of the ordered pair (Jane, John) but obviously does not apply to (John, Jane). It may be convenient to represent 'is taller than' by an arrow, especially if several children are involved, e.g.

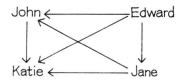

For example, the arrow from Jane to John tells us that Jane *is taller than* John; this is another representation of the fact that (Jane, John) is one of the ordered pairs concerned. The set of all such ordered pairs defines the relationship set up between the pairs of children concerned:

(Edward, John),   (Edward, Jane),
(John, Katie),   (Jane, Katie),
(Edward, Katie), (Jane, John).

*This note is intended for teachers who wish to know more about the properties of the relations that children will discover. It is important but could be omitted at a first reading.

An *equivalence relation* is similarly defined by a set of ordered pairs, but such is the nature of this relation that other ordered pairs may be generated from a few known ones. Suppose, for example, we consider the relation 'works at the same table as'. The ordered pair (Robert, Jane) tells us that Robert works at the same table as Jane. In general we have just seen that order matters, but with this particular relation we can also see that in fact Jane works at the same table as Robert. Thus we may add to the set the ordered pair (Jane, Robert). Here we have a relation such that if the members of the pair are interchanged then the second pair also belongs to the set. A relation having this property is called *symmetric*.

The relation 'is taller than' is not symmetric, since it is clear that if (Jane, John) satisfies the relation then (John, Jane) cannot satisfy it.

Returning to the relation 'works at the same table as', further ordered pairs are implied if we also know that (Jane, Susan) belongs to the set. Because the relation is symmetric we have: (Robert, Jane) implies that (Jane, Robert) belongs to the set and (Jane, Susan) implies that (Susan, Jane) belongs to the set.

A further implication also arises. Since Robert works at the same table as Jane, and Jane works at the same table as Susan, then, clearly, Robert works at the same table as Susan. Hence we have

$$\left.\begin{array}{l}\text{(Robert, Jane)} \\ \text{(Jane, Susan)}\end{array}\right\} \text{implies (Robert, Susan).}$$

A relation possessing this property is called *transitive*. The relation 'works next to' is not transitive. If Peter works next to Paul and Paul works next to Stella, it does not follow that Peter works next to Stella.

Peter   Paul   Stella

We have seen so far that certain relations may be symmetric and others not; that certain relations may be transitive and others not. There is yet another property which is satisfied by some, but not all, relations. A relation is described as *reflexive* if each element concerned has the relationship with itself. Our example of 'works at the same table as' is such a relation. Susan works at the same table as Susan may seem merely a statement of the obvious but it helps to distinguish this type of relation from those which are not reflexive, for example: 'works next to' is not reflexive.

A relation which is

    reflexive,
    symmetric,
    and transitive

is called an *equivalence relation*.

The 'equals' sign

Let us take the set of numbers which we have been discussing, namely {1, 2, 3, 4, . . . }, and the relation 'equals' or '$=$', meaning 'is the same number as'.

1 Any number equals itself (reflexive property; $a=a$), for example, $7=7$. At first sight this may seem a trivial statement because it is so obvious, but is it always obvious? Even the 'seven-ness of 7' is not obvious to infants in the early stages of their experience for we need only remember that, until the concept of conservation has developed, a set of 7 counters when spread out or moved will be counted again to check that there are still 7.

2 Symmetric property: (If $a=b$, then $b=a$)
Here again, this property in respect of numbers becomes obvious only after experience. A child putting pegs into holes sees first that he has the same number of pegs as he has holes. It may not be immediately obvious to him that he has the same number of holes as he has pegs.

3 Transitive property: (If $a=b$ and $b=c$, then $a=c$)
Matching with three sets of objects leads to an appreciation of the transitive property. If four girls are each given a doll, then the number of girls is equal to the number of dolls. If each doll is then put in a cot, the number of dolls equals the number of cots. The final stage is to see that the number of girls is equal to the number of cots.

All three properties:

1. $a = a$ (reflexive),
2. if $a = b$, then $b = a$ (symmetric),
3. if $a = b$ and $b = c$, then $a = c$ (transitive),

are satisfied if a, b, c are numbers, so '=' here gives an equivalence relation.

For the time being, we shall use the symbol '=' to denote only 'is the same number as'. Indiscriminate use of the equality sign and its rules can lead to arguments such as the following:

If 1 penny $= \frac{1}{3}$ ounce
and 1 shilling $=$ 12 pennies
then 1 shilling $= 12 \times \frac{1}{3} = 4$ ounces.

It is true that a penny weighs about $\frac{1}{3}$ oz and that 12 pennies are worth the same as a shilling, but '1 shilling' does not weigh 4 oz.

The trouble here is that the transitive property T is being assumed but '=' is being misused in representing the *different* relations *weighs about, worth the same as*:

The fact that relationships between things may themselves be different in kind and different in behaviour is important.

It is easy enough to convince a child who has made an error such as the example just quoted that his result is wrong; it is not nearly so easy for him to see why it is wrong. We cannot, as teachers, give individual rules for the use of all possible relationships. We can, however, do something better: we can encourage the children to think about relationships from the very beginning. If we do it well and start early enough, the differences between the various kinds of relationship will become so much a part of their mathematical thinking that errors like the above will disappear. Also, and even more important, the children will be able to use their appreciation of relationships to make real sense of those parts of mathematics which are so often now regarded as 'rules of thumb'.

5 Towards measurement

Counting, comparison and matching often arise in the children's work on shape and size, and lead on to measurements.

Measuring girth, circumference, length, width, height of cartons or containers by matching lengths of string will make it easier for a young child to cover them with another material, for example, when he wishes to cover the walls of a doll's house or the cylindrical part of a rocket. With plenty of this type of experience, children's powers of estimation will improve and extend. The children will discover relationships between the sizes of boxes, pieces of wood and card, and will find that when another large thing is needed, sometimes two smaller ones will fit instead. The use of numbers to make comparisons will be demanded in a wide range of practical activities. Number relationships will be revealed in shapes and patterns.

a Needlecrafts

Knitting, sewing and weaving form part of the experience of many young children, boys as well as girls, and much mathematics is inherent in these activities.

Casting on stitches involves counting in ones, but as soon as the purl stitch has been mastered and ribbing attempted, then children frequently need to be able to count in twos – 2 plain, 2 purl, etc., or K.2, P.2.

Later, children will attempt alternate ribbings; for example,

first 4 rows K.4, P.4,
second 4 rows P.4, K.4.

Lengths and widths will be reckoned in rows and stitches.

This produces a pattern which not only demonstrates an inherent fourness but reveals 4^2 as 16.

The children found how many cupfuls of sand the various containers held and recorded pictorially using cup-shapes which they had cut out themselves.

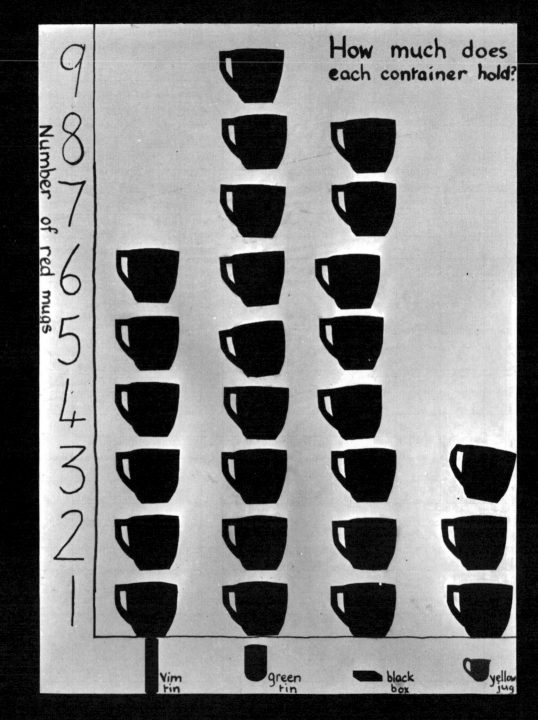

How much does each container hold?

Number of red mugs

9 8 7 6 5 4 3 2 1

Vim tin   green tin   black box   yellow jug

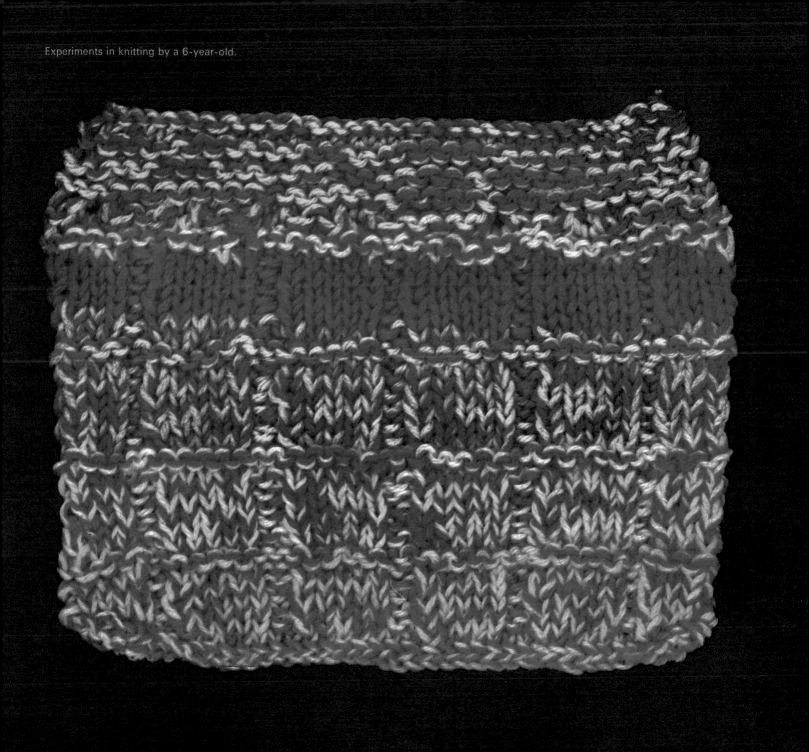
Experiments in knitting by a 6-year-old.

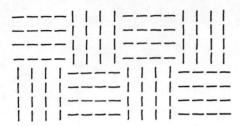

Many children whose skill at knitting is only rudimentary enjoy knitting *squares* and sewing them together to make a blanket for a doll's cot.

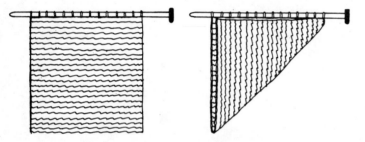

They will learn to fold the knitting over on the diagonal to see *'if it is a square yet'.* When the squares are sewn together, an attractive cot blanket is produced.

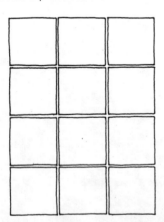

This constitutes an early experience of area, and fitting squares together to cover a surface.

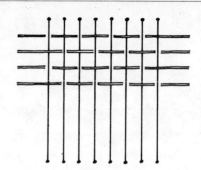

Simple weaving offers experience which will lead to the understanding of *alternate, odd* and *even*.

Later, more skilled pattern weaving will also reveal number patterns.

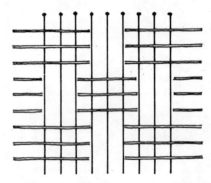

A pattern based on 3

A pattern based on 6
4 and 2
3 and 3

The invention of such patterns should help to reveal number relationships.

Sewing on suitably strong fabric with large needles and gaily coloured thread shows patterns with stitches.

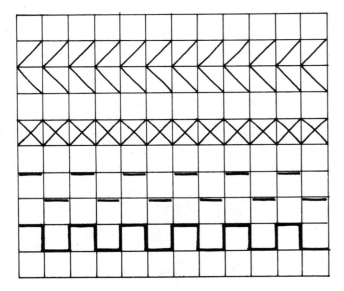

Words that might arise :

    diagonal, alternate, consecutive,
    parallel,
    under, over, front, back, across.

b Imitative play
i Shopping
Shopping is a practical skill and one which every single person must learn for use in life, but mathematics may be drawn out of the concrete experiences. A class 'shop' can help children towards real understanding of number, length, area and volume, if full use is made of opportunities to discuss and talk with the children while they play.

For example, if a child buys six biscuits in the shop, the shop-keeper counts them out for the customer who checks them and puts them into her shopping bag. The teacher can then ask the customer or the shopkeeper how many biscuits there are in the bag. This innocuous question is of course a test of understanding of the invariance of number (cf. p. 24).

After the early, imaginative stages of shopping play the child gradually organises his play more and more as his observations and experience widen. A shop is established with piles of tins, old cartons or toys being used for merchandise. As the understanding of giving something in exchange grows, so buttons or any large quantity of small objects are used for money.

One hears 'a penny for this tin' or 'this toy costs 6p'.

Vocabulary will still not always fit the situation correctly and the child will ask for kilogrammes of bread or eggs, or charge only a few pence for a large doll's pram.

With the increased ability of the children, specific interests arise in school. For example, the children may suddenly develop a great craze to make a shop of their own and fill it with goods they make. The teacher at this time can get quite a large amount of practical work with both money and weighing out of the class-room shop. She can enter into the children's games and buy things from the shop; with a small group she can be 'shopkeeper' for a short time and in so doing help the children with language and vocabulary. She can help with the counting troubles which the children will meet; for example, slower children might be still having difficulty at six years of age when counting out more than ten or twelve objects. They will need some help if two children require to share a number of sweets being sold in the shop.

When children reach this stage of being really capable of constructing their own shop, valuable experience and language can begin at this point in construction.

'Where shall we have the shop? Where is there room to put it? How big do we want it? What shall we use to make the counter? Shall we have a top to it like a market stall?'

Measurement is involved in all this work, the teacher having to take a very active part in the construction.

'What sort of things are we going to sell in the shop? How many different types of, for example, sweets? How many of each shall we make? We need a greater number of small things and a lesser number of larger things. What prices shall we give to the things we have made?'

This is a good opportunity to introduce some kind of weighing device. If there has been a weighing or balancing table in the room, the children will have gained some ideas about balance, but these ideas will still be rather confused. One only has to watch children of 7+ still experimenting and discovering with balance scales to realise that although a child of this age can read a card 'Weigh out 6 ounces of beans', this does not necessarily mean that when he accomplishes the task correctly he has really understood what he has done or is able to explain how he has done it.

The play experiences might lead to suggestions such as 'Let's make another shop next door or a bank to get the money changed', while the mathematics side can lead to work cards based on shop prices, requiring recording of articles bought, prices paid and change received. It can also lead to graph work, using columns.

Prices in our shop:

3p 6p 10p 20p

Later thus:

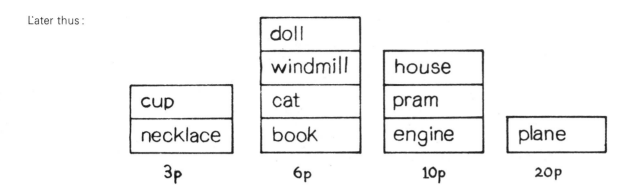

Graphs can also be made of the daily or weekly takings, popularity of items bought or number of children using the shop on each day of the week.

Mapping techniques (cf. p. 42) might also be used in the later stages of shop play.

A 'cut-price' week could be recorded thus:

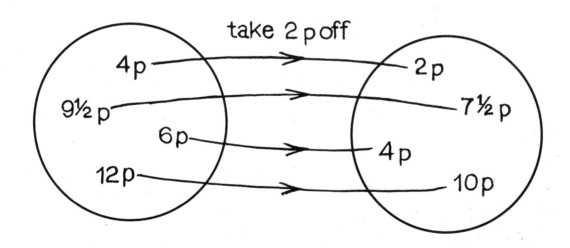

A price list could be shown like this:

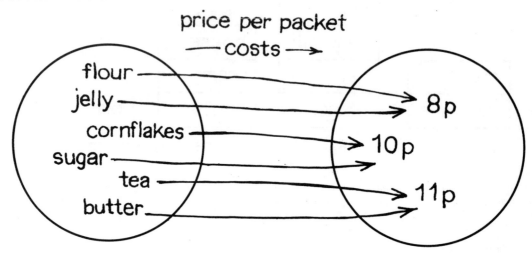

price per packet

— costs →

flour — 8p
jelly —
cornflakes —
sugar — 10p
tea —
butter — 11p

Suggestions for classroom shops

Greengrocer's

Heavy vegetables and fruits can be made from clay or Plasticine cores with paper pasted in layers over the top. Lettuces, greens and cabbages can be made from a ball of newspaper with leaves of crepe or tissue paper pasted on the outside.

Small self-service shops, supermarkets and markets

Various interests can merge into the more contemporary type of shop and children living near a street market or in a market town would be very familiar with the latter. If there is spare space, a room, or part of the hall or corridor could be used. Old bags and baskets, or boxes with wire handles, can be provided and the children can serve themselves, a particularly able child being cashier.

Jeweller's

Children enjoy making necklaces, bracelets and rings from Plasticine, clay or paper beads threaded on to cotton. Macaroni can be used in the same way and then painted. Clocks and watches can be made by the children from card and paper discs.

ii Cooking

This is an imitative activity in the first instance, and children will play at 'cooking' long before they are actually capable of doing anything real about it. Free and varied play with clay and dough mixture will give children opportunities to cut and roll a pliable material and realise the conservation of mass as shape changes. Sometimes it is useful to allow the children to mix their own dough (and clay, also, if the powdered type is used), as mixing is a physical skill which young children find difficult. When a teacher decides that her children would benefit from cooking real cakes, and that they are ready and able to tackle this activity, it is easier if the number of children is limited to about six.

Simple recipes are best to begin with. For example, Fairy Cakes:

8 oz flour
4 oz fat
4 oz sugar
1 or 2 eggs
milk to mix

Seven-year-olds are able to adapt the proportions of a recipe like this; if they find that they have only 2 oz fat, they are able to work out the correct weight of other ingredients.

Small cakes or buns are easier to bake than a single large cake, but with experience the teacher and children will find all sorts of cookery possible, e.g. pancakes on Shrove Tuesday.

Even if no cooking facilities are available, one can still make, for example, chocolate truffles.

Ingredients

2 oz butter,
3 heaped dessertspoonfuls sweetened chocolate powder,
1 heaped dessertspoonful icing sugar.

Method

Mix together and roll into balls on a plate sprinkled with chocolate powder.

The cost of our cakes
6 ozs of flour   3d
3 ozs margarine   4d
3 ozs of sugar   2 d.
  egg   4 d.
4 tablespoons milk   1 d
pinch of salt.   —
cherries   1d
electric   1 d.
                      1s.. 4d.

We made 16 cakes so they were 1d each.

Cooking the cakes.
We put them in the oven at 25 past 11 and they were ready at 10 to 12..

They took 25 minutes.

Mathematical experience which may be gained

Experience of volume, capacity, weighing, estimation, measurement of time; the appreciation of the approximate nature of measurement, and the need for standard units — all these may be derived from cooking activities.

As in the example on p. 63, children may find the prices of the ingredients and work out the cost of each small cake. If there is no 'pinger' available, the children will have to watch the clock; and if an electric oven is used with a small thermometer, the children may notice the temperature at different settings.

An important experience that the children can gain when engaged in cooking is the way in which fractions are used 'conversationally'. For example, the children will soon use the words 'half' and 'quarter' when referring to a mass, or an amount of sugar or fat. It can be seen that a few grains of sugar or a tiny amount of fat scraped from the wrapping paper will not alter the position of the scales or balances, so that the 'half' of fat or sugar is an approximation and should not, and cannot, be identified with the $\frac{1}{2}$ that children are going to meet much later on in their mathematical life, when it will then be an absolute. When children have mixed their ingredients and put the mixture into bun tins, they will have experienced the approximate sharing of a 'measured' quantity. However, when the cakes are cooked the children will be able to share out among each other an exact — 'counted' — quantity, that is, the number of cakes.

Finally, the idea of reversibility is an important one. Cooking provides good counter-examples: it is not possible to start with the Fairy cakes and get back to the ingredients.

iii Home Corner

Many children like and need to play out 'home' situations, for example, in a Home Corner, Wendy House or Hospital Corner. When a group of children have a 'party' they set the table by matching one cup, saucer, plate, etc., to each person long before they count. They share the 'biscuits' or 'cakes' by the same method, until they are all used.

If a large and a small doll are provided, with a set of clothes for each, the children compare sizes and then match the correct clothes to the appropriate doll. A cot and a pram of differing dimensions, with bedding for each, again give opportunities for comparison and matching. Young children find this either difficult or unnecessary at first, but as they grow older they become most particular that things should 'fit'.

The Home Corner dolls can be weighed and measured, this arising very naturally from play as 'mothers' take their babies to the 'clinic'. With one group of children this idea developed into a definite and absorbing interest. They became interested in the shapes made by folding the nurse's head-dress, e.g. it began as a square piece of material but needed to be folded into a triangle to fit the head. They collected Welfare Food containers ('National dried milk' tins, rose-hip syrup, orange juice and cod liver oil bottles) and found out how many feeds or doses could be obtained from each, and for how long each would last before a new one had to be started.

Some young children tried to find as much 'mathematics' as they could in their Home Corner, but soon suggested that if they looked in their own homes they would find much more. They counted the number of people, rooms, chairs, mats, windows, etc. They looked for shapes with which they were familiar from work at school. (See pp. 65-69.)

This might lead to an interest in roads, transport and garages which play such a prominent part in children's lives today. The play and vocabulary involved would be a valuable introduction to later work on speeds, direction, seating, loading, cubic capacity of cars and lorries, fuel consumption, etc. Some young children became very interested in their teacher's car and gained some counting and other experience from their interest. They noticed the registration number and the dials inside and measured width, breadth, height, doors, etc. They could not think of a way of finding the weight of the car, and so those who could read looked in the handbook for that and other information recorded in graphical or other pictorial form.

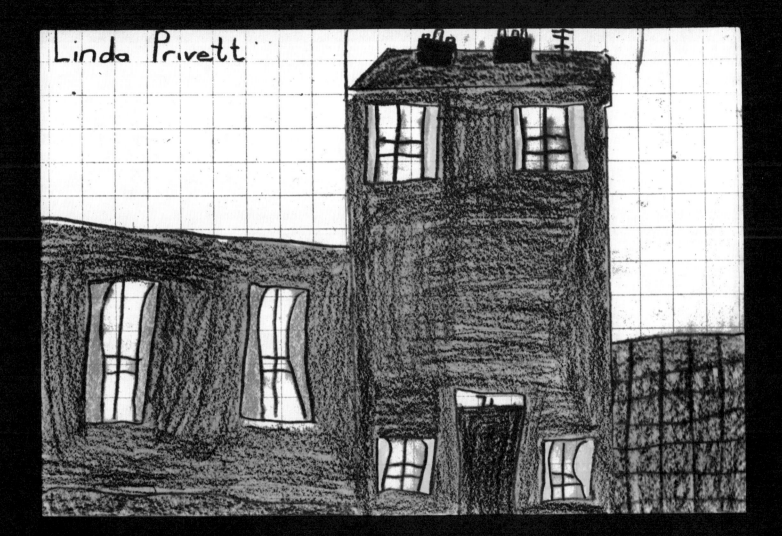

Linda Privett

My windows have 24 panes of glass in the front. I have two windows upstaires and I have two windows downstaires I have one letter-box and I have one door and I have to windows at the side

The Leaves

The following is the teacher's description of this activity.
Leaves of various sizes were left on a table.
'Oh, look at these leaves. Aren't they big? That's a skeleton.'
'This is a big one.'
'This is the biggest.'
'This one is fattest. It's bigger'n yourn.'
'No. This is biggest.'
'I've got one bigger than the others.'
Diana had three beech leaves.
At first she said 'This one is big. Oh, but it's small by yours.'
I said 'Then let us call it small.'
She graded them: small, smaller, smallest.
David had a very wide leaf and a long, narrower one.
He said 'That's fat. That's smaller.'
'What do you mean by fatter?'
'It's bigger – oh no, it's wider.'
He looked at stalks: 'That one's fat – no, I mean thick, and that one's thin.'
Michael had two long sweet-chestnut leaves.
'Mine are tall leaves.'

I had 3. dark red leaves. I put them by the side of David's fat leaf and it made my leaves look small. I put them in a row. small smaller smallest

my little leaves.

David's fat leaf.

Eventually we decided that it was difficult to tell which were 'largest' because one was wider, but one was longer. So we would see how much space they covered. As no one inch square paper was available we resorted to graph paper. The children counted the squares. I watched without comment. Again David said 'There are some bits which don't fill the square. If I make small squares round some they can be a half or a quarter. The other bits will do to make up whole squares.' He counted the squares and made up the halves and quarters correctly and entirely without assistance

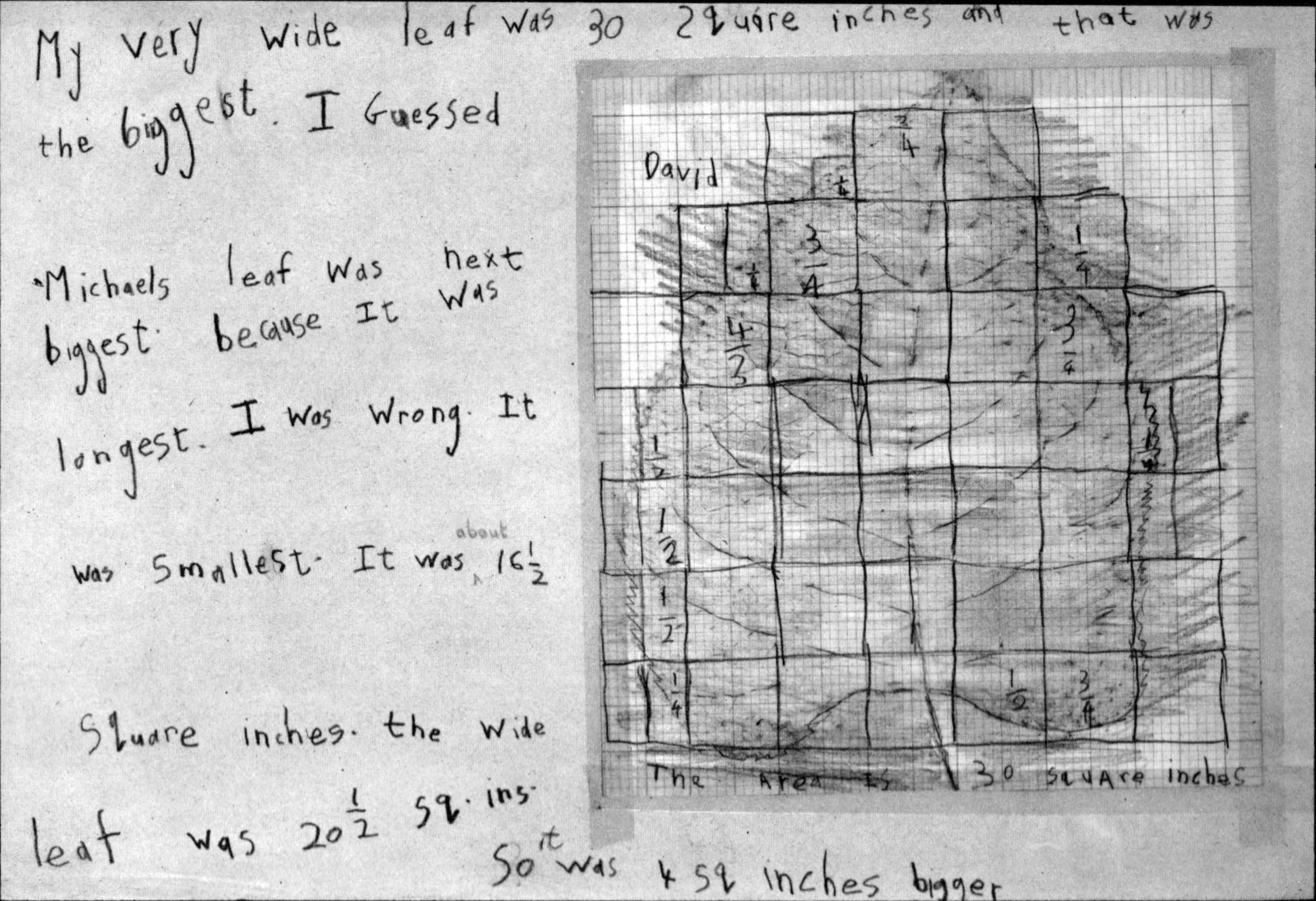

My very wide leaf was 30 square inches and that was the biggest. I Guessed

Michaels leaf was next biggest. because It was

longest. I was Wrong. It

was Smallest. It was about 16½

Square inches. the Wide

leaf was 20½ sq. ins.

So it was 4 sq inches bigger

David

The Area is 30 square inches

I drew round a leaf to see what the
perimeter measured. I tried to measure
with a ruler but the ruler was
too straight. Then I tried
with a thin strip of paper
too straight
but The paper was
and too teary. Then I tried elastic bands

6 Development of vocabulary and mathematical experience

a Balance and weight

Early experiences in this field include such activities as playing on a see-saw and walking along a wall or a balancing bar. These activities involve the use of the child's own body. When materials are used, some kind of balancing device is needed. In the first instance it is advisable to have available a wide range of improvised balances.

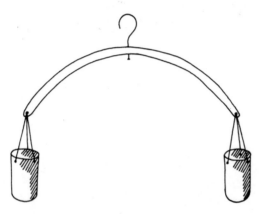

A balance contrived from coat-hangers and tins suspended firmly.

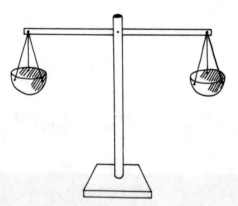

A balance on a firm wooden base. (These can be obtained commercially or improvised.)

Matching and comparison

Given a wide variety of materials, children will enjoy making things balance. This is yet another example of matching. They will eventually find a pebble that will balance a cotton reel, but in the course of their investigation it will be the *inequalities* that arise first — one thing being heavier than the other.

Recording might be attempted in this way:

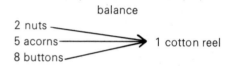

balance
2 nuts
5 acorns ⟶ 1 cotton reel
8 buttons

The relation 'balance' here means 'weighs the same, as near as I can see'.

Ordering

Children might next attempt putting things in order according to their weight. Provision of materials should now include:
i some assorted parcels, differing in size, shape and weight, there being no obvious relationship between size and weight; and on another occasion:
ii some seemingly identical containers, each of a different weight.

This is a difficult task for a child, and his success or failure will give clear indication to the teacher of the level of development of the child attempting it.

We played with the sand out in the hall I had the wet sand I put some wet sand on the scales and it was heavier than Deborah's dry sand. I put two spoonfuls of sand and Deborah put four spoonfuls of sand and the scales balanced

Wendy Parker

If the containers are identified in some way, for example by colour, letter, or number, the children might record their experiences in one of the following ways:

is heavier than

Parcels (4) → (3) → (1) → (2) → (5)

is lighter than

Tins (B) → (A) → (D) → (C)

is heavier than

Containers

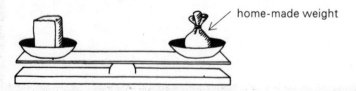

Improvised weights

The first weights the children use should be improvised ones, balanced against real commodities. Children need a large range of bags made from some strong material such as coarse linen or canvas, a wide variety of materials with which to fill them, and some elastic bands.

Starting from something very familiar, such as a pound of sugar, children may then make their own pound weights by filling the bags and securing them with an elastic band.

home-made weight

They will discover for themselves that they cannot necessarily infer the weight of an object from its size.

Each of these weighs about a pound though they all look very different.

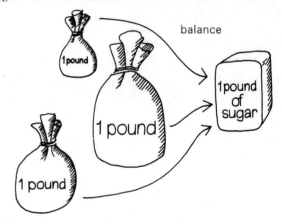

balance

On another occasion the children might use Plasticine to balance a quarter pound of tea. Experiments might evolve the following way, though recording is by no means essential.

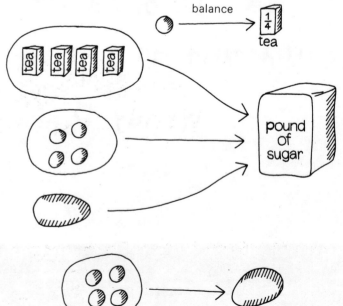

balance

The approximate nature of measurement

It is necessary to highlight the fact that all measurement is by its very nature approximate. Somehow children must be enabled to understand that scales do not give readings that are 'right' or 'wrong', but that the degree of accuracy varies from one pair of scales to another.

This can be achieved through discussion and experiment with everyday commodities. A quarter-pound packet of tea will roughly balance a 4-ounce weight on most school scales. The children are ready to accept that this represents a quarter of a pound to an exact degree: when a few tea-leaves are removed and there is no noticeable difference in the balance of the scales, the children are surprised. Through this and many other similar investigations they will understand that when they weigh a pound it means as near to a pound as one can get with the materials and devices available.

The fact is that no two objects are *exactly* of the same weight (though they may appear to be until a very sensitive balance is used). This is perhaps one of the reasons why the acquisition of the concept of invariance of weight is difficult.

Standard weights

Eventually strong scales and approved standard weights will be found necessary. Sometimes the need will arise during 'general activities' concerning balance; more frequently it will emerge during home play, shop play or cooking.

Even with a wealth of preliminary experience behind them children will still need considerable help before they fully understand the relationships between weights. Fortunately the adoption of decimal coinage and metric measures will make the recognition of relationships between units much easier for children to understand.

Investigations might proceed along these lines, balancing standardised objects against standard weights.

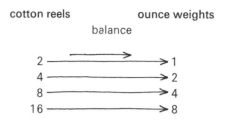

cotton reels   ounce weights
balance

A few children may even detect the pattern that emerges from these numbers.

But of course 'balance' again means 'weighs the same, as near as I can see' so the pattern could well show an irregularity.

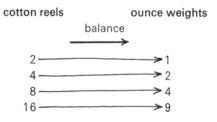

cotton reels   ounce weights
balance

b Volume and capacity

Young children who have had varied and plentiful play with sand, water and bricks will begin to relate their experiences and vocabulary of volume and capacity to other situations as they arise in the environment.

Rather than take the children too quickly into the use of 'standard measurement', that is, before they have discovered the need for it through their own experiences, it is possible to extend the classroom environment.

Materials for additional experience

A selected set of containers is extremely valuable. They may be chosen for the following reasons:

i because some fit well inside others;

ii because some show a definite ordering relation – tall, taller, tallest; or 'one holds twice as much as another';

iii because some hold about as much as others, although this is not readily apparent;

iv because altogether they provide examples of a wide range of shape of container – cubical, rectangular, cyclindrical, elliptical, conical, hexagonal.

In this more structured situation children can discover relationships as well as some characteristics of shapes.

A wide variety of experiences and material produced the interesting piece of work reproduced on p. 75.

This work was leading towards an idea of density, shown by the thoughts of a child who could not yet write fluently on her own.

'I told Mrs Dadd that tea was the lightest because it came from leaves and sand was the heaviest because it came from rocks.'

The 'standard' in this piece of work need not have been a pint; it could have been any mug or jar.

After much comparison of capacity of containers by measuring space inside by counting spoonfuls of material, or by weighing it, children may be encouraged to discover a method to decide which container holds most without using scales and spoons.

Perhaps the first stage is to find out that

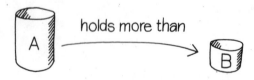

because the material runs over when transferred from A to B.

The children might find that

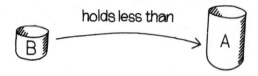

because the material in B will not fill A.

The next stage may be:

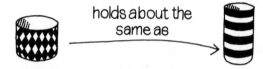

because the material neither runs over nor fails to fill a container when transferred from one to another.

To give children some experience which will bring them towards 'invariance of volume', it may be helpful to provide a number of boxes of different shape, but which all hold, for example, 36 cubes. It is important at this stage that a child should understand that when two containers hold about the same amount of material, we can say that the 'amount of space inside them' (i.e. volume) is about the same. With much more 'filling and fitting' experience, the children will come to understand that no matter how or where the 36 cubes are arranged, they will always take up the same amount of space.

Although children may have weighed the filling materials at some stage to decide upon the size of a particular tin or box, they will have been using their own methods of assessing volume or cubic capacity. Through all this varied experience they come to see the need for some standardisation of cubic and fluid measurement. It is not until they have discovered for themselves the need for its use, and when it has become meaningful to them, that they should be encouraged to use it.

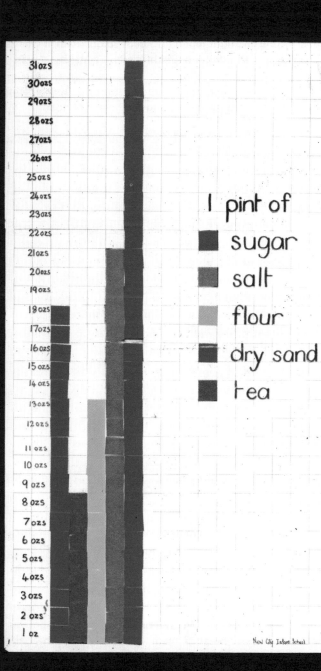

I pint of

sugar

salt

flour

dry sand

tea

1 pint jug

David Bedos
We wondered if they
would all weigh the
same and they did not
weigh the same and the
sand was in the lead because
it was 31 ozs and the tea
8 ozs was at the bottom

c Length and area

Matching and comparison

The most attractive and valuable piece of equipment at this stage is a box of gaily coloured ribbons and strings, all varying in length and thickness.

The problem might be posed: 'See if you can find three things that are as long as your ribbon'.

Here 'as long as' means 'the same length, as near as I can see'.

Children will discover for themselves that a piece of ribbon is a very useful measuring device in that it can be used *up, down, across* and *around.* These words should arise in the discussion of the work.

measuring materials

Here are two examples of the kind of recording that might result from this experience.

i Things that are as long as my ribbon:

 the back of my chair
 the cupboard door
 the side of the milk crate.

ii My ribbon went across the back of my chair, along the side of the milk crate and right round my head. I didn't think it was as far round my head as along the side of the milk crate, but it was.

The children have been concerned so far only with comparing in order to match, the standard being their piece of ribbon.

Many children will move naturally into the next stage of this work by such remarks as:

My ribbon *is longer than* Mary's.

This kind of comment is a useful indicator to the teacher as to the advisability of proceeding to the next stage.

Ordering

Again using the box of ribbons, children might be asked:
i to find the shortest ribbon,
ii to find the longest ribbon,
iii to sort out all the ribbons in order of size
beginning with the shortest,
beginning with the longest.

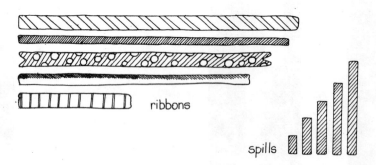

ribbons

spills

Very few children at this level will be able to solve this problem of size-order quickly. Most of them will tackle it on the basis of comparison of two lengths, then a further two, and so on.

More suggestions
Waist measurements

Using cheap ribbon or tape each child in the group cuts off the piece of tape that measures round his waist. These are then compared and placed in size-order. They could be stuck on to paper or card for a permanent record, e.g.

Right round our waists

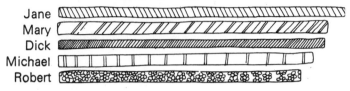

Jane
Mary
Dick
Michael
Robert

Covering surfaces

In the course of natural play in the classroom there will arise experiences preliminary to the notion of area.

The dressing-up box will contain a dress that is too *long* for Julia. There will be pieces of material deemed to be too *small* for cloaks or too *big* for veils. To the children there is simply too much or too little material for their purpose. Mathematically it is not that any particular dimension is excessive or deficient but that the total area is inappropriate.

Children have many opportunities for covering surfaces such as putting a table cloth on a table or a cover on a cot. Others are more complex involving more careful matching and measuring. When children are making models using junk materials, they come across the need to cover surfaces which are not flat, and not limited to the horizontal or vertical plane, and this provides valuable experience.

The word *surface* sometimes causes difficulty, but there are occasions when its meaning becomes more readily apparent.

Roads and playgrounds get resurfaced.

'Water-lilies covered the surface of the pond.'
'The frog rose to the surface.'

The role of the teacher is not only to make provision for this kind of experience but to discuss it with the children in order to ensure that, in time, they will be able to understand and use the phrase *covering a surface.*

Distance, direction, perimeter and circumference

At this stage the range of measuring materials can include some that are rigid as well as many that are flexible, e.g. laths, bamboo sticks, garden canes, spills, as well as ribbons, tapes and string; now there will be a need for counting. In order to investigate the distance across the classroom the children will first have to choose suitable materials and then count how many they have used, e.g. having selected a bunch of garden canes, to count how many are needed to stretch across the classroom floor. In this context it is possible to extend vocabulary:
across indicates *direction,*
from one side to another indicates *distance.*

The teacher must ensure that the children's experience of measuring is not confined to the horizontal plane. They need to experiment in as many directions as possible. When measuring the height of a cupboard they should be encouraged to measure from the top down as well as from the ground up.

In order to measure round a ball, a milk bottle, a finger or a waist, the children will select string or ribbon. They will discover that these materials will also be of value in measuring round a book or a box. After plenty of experience they will have no difficulty in using the precise vocabulary – *perimeter* and *circumference.*

In children's words: 'Measuring round a tin is measuring round a circle. It has no straight sides or corners. We call this circum-ference'.

'Measuring round a book is like measuring round the edge of a rectangle. It has corners and straight sides. This is perimeter.'

It is significant that children seem to find no difficulty in the use of these words, for they are precise and unambiguous.

'All the way round'

measuring round a tin – *circumference*

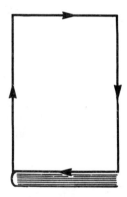

measuring round a book – *perimeter*

Improvised units
Units of length

It was suggested earlier that the height of a cupboard should be measured both from the top down as well as from the ground up. A group of children might work together measuring the width of a cupboard, one pair working from left to right, the other from right to left.

They might repeat the experiment using different materials. One pair might use garden sticks, the other a packet of spills.

Recording could be in the following form:

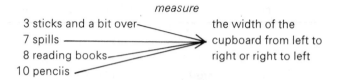

This kind of experience is valuable in many ways, not least of which is to help to clarify the words *left* and *right* which cause great difficulty to many children.

The discovery that 7 spills placed end to end seem to cover approximately the same distance as '3 and a bit' sticks leads to further discussion concerning small and large units. This introduces a new kind of matching experience.

Here 5 spills are matched against 1 garden cane.

Here 4 matchboxes are matched against 1 spill to cover approximately the same distance.

Children need many opportunities of this kind before they begin to appreciate the relationship that exists between

It is far more difficult for a child to measure the distance across his table using handspans than using spills. He simply has to lay out the spills end to end so that they stretch across the table and then count them. If he is using spans, then he needs to count the number of times he can stretch out his hand to reach across the table – a far more complicated process.

Some children discovered that the span of their hands was the 'same' since they got the same answer when they counted the number of spans across the table.

Other occasions will give different answers when two different feet, perhaps a child's and a teacher's, are used to measure across a classroom. This will highlight the need for a standard *foot*.

Units of area

Initially children seem happiest handling three-dimensional units to cover surface area. They will discover how many matchboxes they need to cover the surface of their reading books, how many reading books are necessary in order to cover the surface of the table. Stocking boxes, handkerchief boxes are all useful for this work and many stores will co-operate and supply them. At a later stage the children will use paper of all kinds: school paper, paper bags, sheets of newspaper, as units for covering surface area.

Perimeter and area

It is frequently noted that children find difficulty in establishing the difference between the notion of *perimeter* and that of *area*. Sound early experiences should be contrived in such a way that children can establish the idea that a boundary or hoop encloses area.

How many balls can we fit inside a school hoop? What can we do about the gaps?

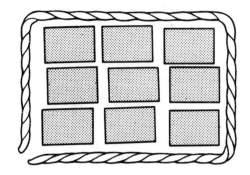

A skipping rope in the shape of a rectangle.
How many stocking boxes can we fit inside?
What can we do about the spaces?
Could we get more in if we moved the rope a bit?

Discussion should spark off this kind of question, and should help towards the eventual establishment of the notions of distance, circumference, perimeter and area.

Standard units

When children find the need for standard measures, then and only then should these be introduced.

Units of length

The following materials might be found useful at this stage:

foot sticks
i unmarked
ii marked in inches (some with alternate colours and others with the numerals shown);

metre sticks
i unmarked
ii marked in centimetres;

yard sticks
i unmarked
ii marked in inches
iii marked in feet
iv marked in half-yards
v marked in quarter-yards;

trundle wheels
circumference 1 yard and 1 metre ;

tape measures
marked in inches or centimetres only,
made from tape or strips of Fablon backing.

Units of area
The following materials might be found useful at this stage :

inch squares and   i   home-made,
centimetre squares   ii   transparent — commercially provided ;
foot squares   i   made from cardboard or linoleum,
               ii   polystyrene tiles ;
metre squares   made from strong wrapping paper,
and yard squares   old corrugated paper or linoleum.

Recording
Confusion is caused by the premature introduction of the short-hand symbols :

   yd   ft   in
   ×   '   "

or even worse :

   sq. yds   sq. ft   sq. ins

Such recording as is found desirable should either be in the child's own words and involve the use of yard, square foot, etc., or be diagrammatic :

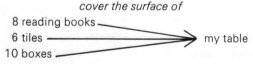

cover the surface of
8 reading books
6 tiles   →   my table
10 boxes

d   Symmetry. Shape and size
To a young child the world is three-dimensional, composed of many objects differing in colour, texture, shape and size. Many of these objects or groups of objects are symmetrical in some way.

A study of children's drawings and paintings frequently reveals what could be described as 'instinctive symmetry'. Illustrations are included in order to show that ideas of symmetry are *natural* ideas, and that when it seems appropriate children will have no difficulty in formalising them. (See pp. 82-85.)

Observation
The most important aspect of this work is to encourage in children an awareness of the shapes and patterns around them. This is simply a matter of focusing attention for a few moments, and introducing the necessary vocabulary so that the children can describe what they see. Such brief discussions might concern :

shapes on the floor	clothes being worn
shapes on the ceiling	trees and flowers
doors and windows	cars and buses
books and pencils	walls and railings.

Vocabulary
It is through observation and discussion that vocabulary growth can be fostered. Words arising in this way will include :

   straight, curved, zigzag,
   vertical, horizontal, diagonal,
   round, circle, spiral,
   sphere, cylinder, cube,
   face, edge, corner

and possibly

   cone, prism, cuboid.

Sorting and classifying (cf. p. 12)
As children select from a junk box what they need to make, say, a rocket, many opportunities arise for discussion and the consequent fostering of vocabulary growth and fluency.

In answer to the question 'Why did you choose this tin ?' a child will probably reply, 'Because it's the right shape for a funnel'. This may be the occasion to introduce the word cylinder. On a subsequent occasion it would be possible to return to the subject of cylinders, find all the cylinders in the junk box, and discuss the surface shapes — that the top and bottom are circular — and so on.

Ordering

It is comparatively easy for a child to put a collection of circles in order of size (i.e. area). He can do this first by placing them on top of each other:

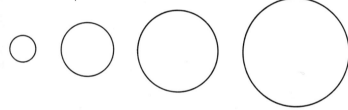

He can then proceed further

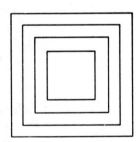

A similar technique is possible with squares

and then

Problems emerge, however, when ordering areas of triangles or rectangles of different shape is attempted.

Some children will not be able to solve this problem for some time. Others who have had plenty of experience of covering surfaces will be able to devise a way of doing it.

Patterns

Young children delight in making patterns using crayon, paint, coloured paper or fabric.

At this stage attention might be focused on the different kinds of patterns observed and described by the children.

Mathematical terms	Children's description
Reflection	back to front
	upside down
Translation	moving along
Rotation	round and round

Axes of symmetry

'Back to front', 'upside down' and 'round and round' could be the means of introducing the idea of an *axis of symmetry*.

All investigations should derive from something familiar within the environment. A collection of square things might include a handkerchief, a table napkin and a headsquare.

'Try folding your handkerchief (or headsquare, etc.) in half in as many different ways as you can.' This is a real problem. These things do get folded.

More rare is this kind of drawing based on the shape of a circle.

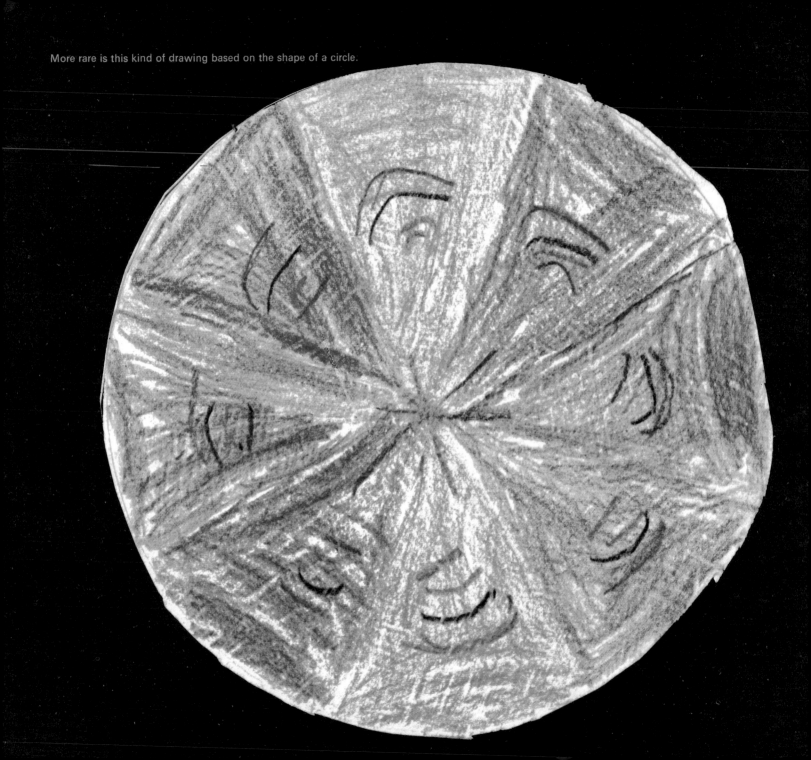

I found some sycamore seedlings. They look like. aeroplane wings

The children might then each cut out a piece of paper to match the article they are working with, fold it again, and mark the lines of the fold.

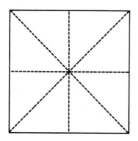

The four folds represent four axes of symmetry.

A circle could be folded in the same way, to make a paper doily.

'Back to front' designs are based on a *vertical* axis

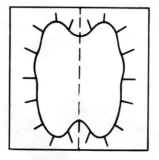

'Upside down' based on a *horizontal* axis

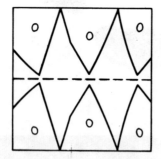

Some designs have *horizontal* and *vertical* axes

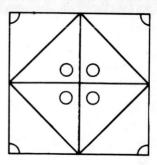

A crossways design is based on a *diagonal* axis

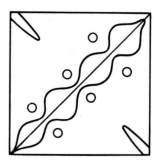

e Time
The notion of time
Few people will dispute that children have 'no idea of time'; they live exclusively in the present. Only as they mature do they realise that each moment is joined to the next, that time is continuous and never ending. Nevertheless, children can be given experiences of *time passing* and *timing*.

The vocabulary of time
One of the first 'time words' to become meaningful to a child is *now* with its opposite *not now*, although the latter can refer to the past or the future. The *day* is perhaps the first *measure* of time to have some meaning. *Today* is made up of a succession of events — the *morning* is getting-up, having breakfast, Daddy going to work, going to school, etc.

'We'll go out after dinner' is understood sooner than 'We'll go out this afternoon' or 'at half-past two'.

A child who is used to some kind of routine will come to understand parts of the day, and even *times* of the day, through the continuing regularity of the days.

The days and weeks of the immediate present are named within a span of five and are in colloquial use:

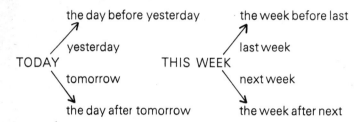

the day before yesterday   the week before last

yesterday   last week

TODAY   THIS WEEK

tomorrow   next week

the day after tomorrow   the week after next

However, the way in which a child himself uses the words both in speech and later in written work will give some guide as to the extent of the understanding he has. The names of the days of the week and the months of the year slowly become memorable when they are related to events within the child's life. The birth month is often learned first; December is linked with Christmas, November with Guy Fawkes; August is the month when school is closed.

Timing and time passing

Experiences which can give 'time' some meaning for young children are those concerned with timing and time passing. Timing is the process by which we measure a span of time.

A beginning can be made by measuring the duration of a well-known situation, then comparing this with new situations or experiences; for example, the time it takes for one child to walk the length of the hall; then walking the same distance with a heavy box; then comparing the times of other children (see p. 88). The children will think of many other experiments of this kind: the time taken to hop, jump, skip with rope, walk backwards, walk with eyes shut, etc., across the length and breadth of hall or playground, or round them; the time taken to go up and down stairs, on journeys to school for both children and teachers.

For the measurement of these times it is preferable for the children to think of their own measuring device; it might be a sand clock, a water clock, a steadily dripping tap, counts of their pulse, egg-timers or, for older children, candle clocks.

Very simple sand clock

Ice-cream cornet pierced over jam jar.

Time taken for cakes to bake, time allowed on large P.E. apparatus, time for lunch break, etc., can be observed and recorded.

Telling the time

This is simply dial-reading, but nevertheless a skill which some children find much easier than others.

The times that children will learn first are those related to an event. '1 o'clock' will be at first another *name* for dinner-time and the position of the hands on the clock will be recognised to coincide with the meal. 'Bed-time' gives another position of the hands on the clock that will soon be recognised.

f   Number

There is no such concrete thing as 'two'; it is a useful notion describing experiences. The work outlined in this section will offer children many opportunities to use number words in a descriptive way, and so will help towards establishing the idea of number.

Counting

Counting opportunities arise naturally in almost every field of activity. The children will find the need to count how many cotton reels, foot-sticks, ounces or whatever they have been using. If they measure using their own feet they will need to count the number of times they put their feet down heel to toe.

David Perry

It took Allan 50
seconds to walk 95
yards. It took Allan
less time because
he has longer
legs.

Fractions

Children hear and use the word *half* before they come to school. They are given *half* a cake, or someone says 'I'll cut this apple in *half*'. They hear people refer to a *quarter* of tea, and will tell you proudly that they are 'four and *three quarters*'.

Fractions are in everyday use in connection with almost all the common units of mass :

quarter pound	half pound	three quarters of a pound
quarter ounce	half ounce	three quarters of an ounce
a quarter of a yard	half a yard	three quarters of a yard

but never a quarter of a foot or half a foot.

Opportunities will arise in a variety of situations for children to discover the relationship between the parts and a whole. The 'halves', 'quarters', 'three-quarters' of this context are colloquial approximations, not exact mathematical entities.

Operations

i Addition

Natural opportunities for 'addition' arise in many ways. For example, there is commonly no three-ounce weight so children will find the equivalent using a two-ounce and a one-ounce weight. To weigh five ounces they will find several possibilities :

one and one and one and one and one,
four and one,
two and two and one.

Altogether is the key word at this stage. Each of these combinations of weights, altogether, produces the required weight, five ounces.

Opportunities to foreshadow the relationship between addition and subtraction will also arise naturally.

Children measuring across a table 2 feet wide, and finding a yard stick too long may discover relationships between 1, 2 and 3.

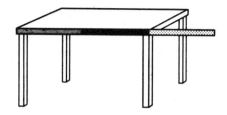

This is an early experience that will lead to the eventual understanding of subtraction as the inverse of addition.

ii Division and multiplication

Given a bag of sweets, a young child will find a way to *share* it between himself and two friends. He *matches* one sweet to each child, then another, then another and so on until the bag of sweets is empty.

one sweet each
then another
then another
and so on.

The interesting thing is that frequently the child discovers that he has one or two sweets left over. This is the first experience of what is later conventionally known as a remainder.

To give the child experience of *repeated subtraction* the question would have to be

'How many children can each have three sweets from this bag ?'

The child will then remove three, then another three, then another three and so on. In this instance too he may well find he has one or two left over.

then another   then another

left over

These two aspects of division, *sharing* and *repeated subtraction* are both important.

Children are frequently asked to 'share this' between them. They might share a length of ribbon while 'dressing up'. This is a real experience of 'finding a half'.

A draper's shop with rolls of ribbon will provide opportunities for repeated subtraction, cutting ten-centimetre lengths from the roll.

Multiplication in this context is *repeated addition* and again the word *altogether* is significant. To produce a six-ounce weight children might use three two-ounce weights, giving six ounces *altogether*.

Patty pans used for baking cakes show useful patterns. The most common ones make provision for six, nine or twelve cakes or tarts.

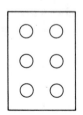

three rows of two
two rows of three

three rows of three

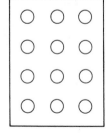

four rows of three
three rows of four

On p. 78 children discovered that five spills could be matched against one garden cane. This experience could be extended to give children problems concerning multiplication and division.

spills		garden canes
5	→	1
10	→	2
15	→	3
20	→	4
garden canes		spills
1	→	5
2	→	10
3	→	15
4	→	20

Number bases
The experience described above involves five little units being in some way equivalent to one large unit, an early introduction to a number base of five. The measure of six spills could be interpreted as | |

garden canes   spills

| |

This kind of occasion arises again with the introduction of standard measures. Nine pints could be recorded as

gallons   pints

| |

the number base being eight.

Recording
The essence of this work is experience and discussion. When recording is found desirable it would be best to use pictorial representation, i.e. picture, block graph or diagram, or the child's own words.

7 A brief review

The suggestions made in Part III are based on the belief that mathematics for young children derives from and returns to a stimulating classroom environment where it will be fed and nourished by natural curiosity. *Balance* and *symmetry* are at the heart of mathematics and many of the natural play experiences of childhood seem instinctively to reach towards these notions. Much of the work involves *matching* and *comparison*, and discussion makes possible the discovery of *relationships*, numerical and spatial.

Work of this nature cannot be restricted to a fixed period on a timetable. Much of it will require long periods of time to be available, for it naturally spills over from and into language work and all forms of creative activity. Indeed the work would be barren were this spill-over not possible.

The activities described in this book should foster the growth of 'mathematical insight'. This is not primarily a matter of remembering facts or manipulating numbers, but rather of the ability to perceive relationships. It is this ability that a teacher must try to identify.

Great problems arise in the evaluation of progress. Sometimes children can understand things but cannot communicate their understanding. In other children, glib verbal facility would lead one to assume understanding that does not in fact exist.

A child who can look at the following information
          8 reading books
          6 tiles ⟶ my table
          10 stocking boxes
and suggest that the relation could be
                    cover the surface of
is showing a considerable mathematical insight.

The symbol → is a very widely used one, indicating a relationship between the objects connected by it. It can express a correspondence between members of two sets. The particular correspondence varies from one situation to another, e.g. above it is 'covers the surface of'; elsewhere it may be 'belongs to', 'is greater than' and so on.

The idea of *mapping* is important since it is often desirable that given a member of a first set we *know* the corresponding member of the second set. But children may encounter other correspondences. For example, children experimenting with a balance might record their findings in this way :

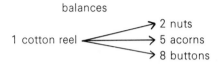

balances

1 cotton reel ⟶ 2 nuts
          ⟶ 5 acorns
          ⟶ 8 buttons

since they actually started with a cotton reel. This is not a mapping because more than one arrow leaves the element of the first set. The correspondences we have considered, whether mappings or not, have been concerned with the relation between the elements of two sets. Relationships are all-important.

8 Representation

We turn now to graphical representation and consider its value in revealing hitherto unsuspected relationships.

Graphs give information in a concise form

A graph simplifies masses of figures, statements and calculations. It may also permit us to see trends, etc., not easily observed in the original data.

Graphs communicate and the communication must be interpreted. Therefore children should be encouraged to have discussions on them and produce a 'White Paper' (short comments) to accompany the graph. The 'White Paper' may be the comments of one child who is preparing an individual piece of work; or, if it is a group project, the comments of each child can be arranged in booklet form.

Graphs show relationships

Probably the most important value of graphs, and one which applies especially to the pupils of lesser ability, is that they help children to see relationships which may have passed by unnoticed. This is important because mathematics is the study of relationships. It is the interrelationships between the facts of arithmetic rather than the facts themselves which command attention. As these relationships are seen and discussed, concepts become clearer, and fundamental principles will emerge.

It is essential that children should be given frequent opportunities to record and communicate their experiences in graphical forms.

Graphs provide data for computation

In the discussion of a pictorial representation a teacher can draw out the need for computation. Eventually the child will produce problems from graphs not only for himself but to test his friends.

Here are some examples:

Where we all Come from.

Miles Green | Scot Hay | Alsagers Bank | Halmer End | Audley

I live at Miles Green.

Most Children in our class Come from miles Green It is the smallest village.

A lot of new houses have been built at Scot Hay and 5 Children Come from there.

Halmer End is the biggest village. but there are a lot of old houses and old people living there.

One boy comes from Audley. Audley is a long way from our School and they have a School there as well.

26 Children in our class.

$8+6+6+5+1=26.$

S Procter.

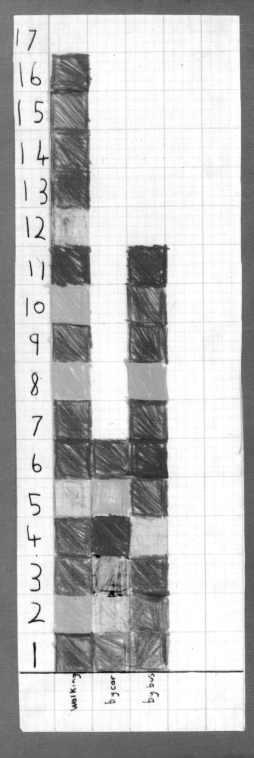

17
16
15
14
13
12
11
10
9
8
7
6
5
4
3
2
1

walking | by car | by bus

Types of representation

From the block charts shown on pp. 33, 34 and above, in which each object is represented by a 'block', children can now move on to more abstract representation.

Richard   7 years.

The graph tells us that most people walk home from school. It tells you that eleven people come by bus. It tells you that 6 people come by car. It tells you that there are 33 people in the class. It tells you that 10 more people walk home than go by car. And 5 more people come by bus than by car. And it shows you that 5 more people walk home from school than go by bus

a   Bar charts

Instead of drawing separate symbols, long rectangles (bars) of the same width can represent the data. It is the length (height) of the column which 'catches the eye' and gives the information required. Sometimes the columns are separated, the points between the bars being meaningless; or the bars may be adjacent. The vertical axis may detail the numbers concerned, or the bars may be drawn to scale, the details being shown below the illustration.

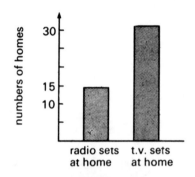

Scale: 1 in. to represent 10 sets.

The height or length tells you on sight that the number of T.V. sets is almost double the number of radio sets. Other examples could be heights, or number of children in a family.

b   Bar line charts

This type of graph is made up of lines instead of rectangles, and the lines may be arranged horizontally or vertically. The numbers concerned are represented by lengths.

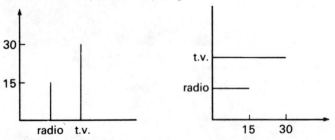

Bar lines are easy to use when approximating and 'rounding off' numbers where decimal parts of an inch or metre are used, e.g. a line to represent 387 people could be drawn 3·9 in long (390 people, 100 people represented by one inch). Examples could be loaves of bread bought one day by a number of families, or bottles of milk Mother buys each day for a week.

These two types are illustrated on pp. 95 and 96 by children's work. Notice how much more sophisticated these are than the 'coloured squares' on p. 34.

Vocabulary

Axis

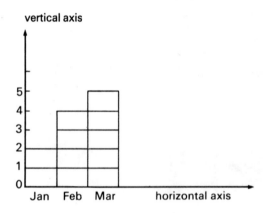

An 'axis' is a start-line. The above illustration is of the number of children in a class born in various months. The vertical axis is marked off with the numbers 0, 1, 2, 3, . . . evenly spaced (with an arrow to show that these numbers can be continued as far as necessary); the horizontal axis too is marked off in equal intervals to represent the months concerned.

Our Pets

In our class there are 14 dogs and 7 cats

14 + 7 = 21., So this is **21** pets

There are more dogs than cats

(14 > 7)

There are twice as many dogs as cats. -

14 = two 7's

14 is three 4's and 2 over.

It is an even number.

7 is two 3's and 1 over.

It is an odd number.

7 is one 5 and 2 over

There are only 17 children who have pets. **3** children have 2 dogs each and 1 boy has 2 cats

21 is three 7's and is an odd number.

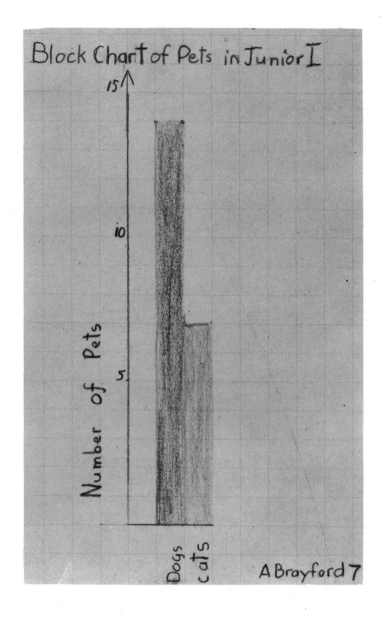

Block Chart of Pets in Junior I

Number of Pets

15
10
5

Dogs cats

A Brayford 7

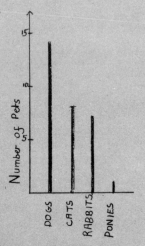

LINE CHART OF PETS IN JUNIOR II.

Number of Pets

DOGS CATS RABBITS PONIES

The children in our class have lots of pets.

There are 14 dogs, 8 cats, 7 rabbits and 1 pony.

Dogs are the favourites. There are 14.

(14 is > 8 > 7 > 1).

The chart shows this.

The number of dogs and the pony is the same as the number of cats and rabbits.

14 + 1 = 8 + 7
15 = 15

A dog will guard the house when you go out and is wellworth the 7/6 you must pay for a licence, the tins of food you must buy for it and the daily exercise you must give it.

Many of us would like a pony but Susan lives on a farm where she can turn the pony out to graze in the summer or keep him in the stable in winter.

E. Humber.   8 years.

Frequency

This is the number of times an event occurs, e.g.

i There were 8 Division 1 soccer teams which scored 2 goals on Saturday. The event was 'a team in Division 1 scored 2 goals on Saturday'.
The frequency of the event was 8.

ii 7 children in our class each have a dog as a pet.
The event : having a dog as a pet.
Frequency : 7.

Tallying

We tally when we represent each passing vehicle by a stroke (/) or a cross (x). The number of times each event occurs (the 'frequency' of the event) and a summary of the data can be arranged like this :

Event (Vehicles passing)	Tally	Frequency (Number)
Lorries	~~////~~ ~~////~~ ///	13
Cars	~~////~~ ////	9

It should be noted that we have counted in fives — four strokes in succession //// with one stroke across them to complete the five : ~~////~~

BLOCK CHART

Lesley Brian. A Histogram of Tickets sold by IA1.

We sold the largest number of tickets on the first day. On the second Wednesday and Friday we sold the same number of tickets. On these two days the smallest number of tickets were sold. We sold 214 tickets altogether. They cost 3d each so we sold £2 11 13 11 6d worth.

Ticket sold (y-axis): 80, 70, 60, 50, 40, 30, 20, 10

Bar values: 49, 25, 27, 13, 21, 13

Days (x-axis): Wednesday, Friday, Monday, Tuesday, Wednesday, Thursday, Friday

Lesley Brian   Questions

How many *more* tickets did we sell on the first Wednesday than we sold on the second Friday? We sold 53 more.

How many tickets *less* did we sell on the last Friday than we sold on first Friday? We sold 36 less

How many *More* tickets did we sell on Tuesday than we sold on Monday? We sold 3 More.

On the first Friday we sold 49 on the Second Friday we sold 13 altogether? We sold 62

Links with science

Mathematics obtains many illustrations from life and the environment, in which living things, whether animal or vegetable, play a considerable part. Some examples are given below.

Children can consider the different shapes to be found in leaves, and then in the classroom use string or tape to measure around them. (See pp. 67–69.) The perimeters can be represented by the actual pieces of string or wire arranged as a bar graph, e.g.

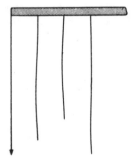

Lengths of string hanging down, representing perimeters of leaves.

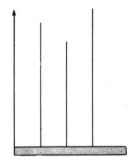

Lengths of wire (held by Plasticine), again representing perimeters of leaves.

with the name of the leaf near the appropriate piece of string. Or the child can cut a strip of cardboard the same length as the string, and arrange the pieces in length order on the desk or stick them on paper.

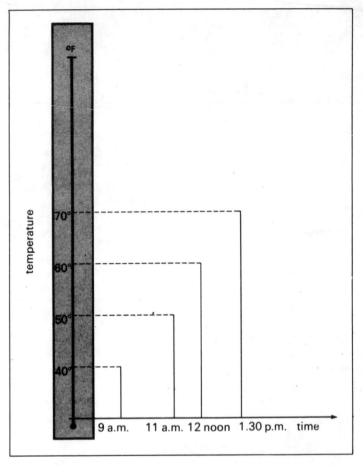

Recording the room temperature is a popular activity. The children use a thermometer placed on a piece of graph paper and mark the height of the mercury or alcohol directly on to the paper. A bar line chart is used to record the temperature, each line corresponding to the height of the liquid.

In fact bar line charts can be used to record a diversity of observations, from the growth of a plant to the changes in length of the tail of a pet mouse.

Care needed

children staying to lunch

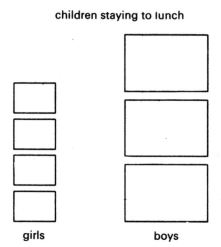

girls   boys

What's wrong with this? Clearly the boxes should be the same size. It looks as though there were more boys than girls, which of course is not true. This section deals with some of the things that can go wrong and some of the places where special care is needed.

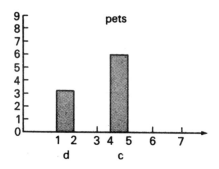

What's wrong with this?
1 There are no titles giving meaning to the horizontal and vertical axes. Does 'd' stand for dogs, ducks, dormice, ... ?
2 An arrow should be shown on the vertical axis following the last number, to show that the numbers could be continued if necessary.
3 Writing in numbers on the horizontal axis is incorrect: only dogs and cats are being considered. The arrow is also misleading.
4 The bars should be evenly spaced, in spite of the fact that the intervals between them are meaningless.

This would have been a better presentation:

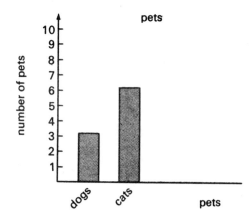

Horizontal axis

Care should be taken when marking this axis.

a Order *not required*

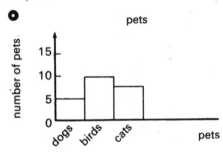

Any order is used. We could have shown the 'bird' column as the first, then the 'cat' column.

Note carefully

i Arrow used with vertical axis. We could have continued to 20, 25, . . . had it been necessary.

ii No arrow used with horizontal axis. We are concerned with sets of dogs, birds, cats, not numbers.

iii Equal intervals used on the horizontal axis.

iv Titles are stated. There is no doubt what our picture is meant to convey.

b Order *required*

The shoe sizes are arranged in order on the horizontal axis. This order assists quick interpretation.

size of shoe	1	2	3	4	5
frequency	0	4	8	3	1

(cf. p. 37)

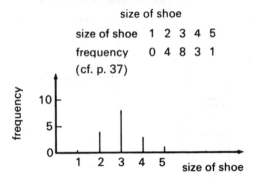

Note carefully

i Arrows on horizontal and vertical axes. More shoe sizes and higher frequencies for a particular size could be shown if data turned up.

ii The title tells what the picture is about.

Be very careful where you label the horizontal axis for a block graph.

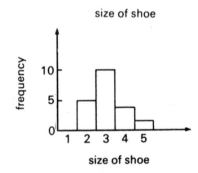

Note the position of the numeral representing each shoe size — near the centre of the rectangle representing the size.

Comparing heights

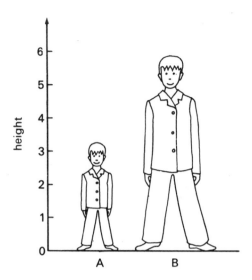

What's wrong with this?
B is *twice* the height of A and this representation is misleading,
for B covers *four* times the surface of A.

When charts are drawn using picture symbols representing area
or volume, they must be observed very closely. A bar line chart
would have been preferable in this case.

Conclusions
Care must be taken to distinguish between what is *certain* from
a graph and what *seems likely*. For example, from one graph it
may be possible to say with certainty

'There are more boys than girls in the class',

but from another graph, on which sales are shown as having gone
up over, say, five months, it would at most be possible to predict

'Sales are *likely* to continue to rise.'

Part IV
Towards a number system

1 Natural numbers

Through experiences of recognising or becoming aware of 'two-ness', 'threeness', etc., in a variety of real situations, the child has learned to attach the appropriate number name to a set of objects. This resembles the way in which man developed this abstract concept of number which he needed to be able to count and record his possessions: cattle, sheep, and crops. Very quickly, no doubt, a standard set was used for matching with a set of real objects and what better at this stage than his fingers or toes? Larger numbers, of course, presented a greater difficulty and it was then that the idea of tallying became a marked step forward: using either notches cut into a piece of wood or knots tied in a piece of fibre.

The historical development of natural numbers and how man first began to write them can be fascinating to young children. It is suggested that stories illustrating the development of *natural* (or, as they are sometimes called, 'counting') numbers be used.

In early days the signs representing a numeral were merely strokes, like those we use in tallying today. These probably represented the fingers of the hand. The word 'digit 'which is a word we use for each of the numerals 1 to 9 comes from the Latin word *digitus*: finger. Should we be surprised when children use their fingers to count?

During the first year or two in school, young children will become familiar with the numbers 1 to 9 and will also recognise 10 as a number, perhaps even 20, 30, 40, etc., but we must realise that at this stage these are only numbers, and there is little or no appreciation of place value. So, during the next stages, work concerning computation will be aimed at acquiring a real understanding of natural numbers, skill in counting natural numbers and the introduction of zero, represented by the symbol 0. Through stories of historical development, with practical illustrations and application where possible, the children will be helped to become aware of our system of notation and place value. The need for an organised structure should also become apparent.

Roman symbols and the Chinese rod numerals show that at one time five was the basis of their counting systems, almost certainly from the number of fingers on the hand. Thus we have: 1, 2, 3, 4, 5, and '5 and 2', '5 and 3', two 5s, 'two 5s and 1', etc.

Roman numerals

I	II	III	IIII	V	
VI	VII	VIII	VIIII	X	XI

Chinese numerals

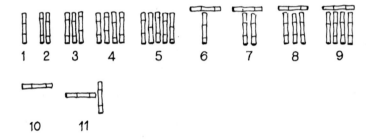

1 2 3 4 5 6 7 8 9

10 11

It was then easy to use both hands and use ten as a base. Ten is used as a base in nearly every part of the world today and we have:

1, 2, 3, 4, 5, 6, 7, 8, 9, 10,

⑪ ⑫ ⑬ ⑭ ⑮
10+1, 10+2, 10+3, 10+4, 10+5,

⑯ ⑰ ⑱ ⑲ ⑳
10+6, 10+7, 10+8, 10+9, Two tens,

It can be seen that we are working towards a convenient system of notation, the idea of place value and the idea of a number base (sometimes called the counting set).

2   The development of weights and measures

'Weights and measures' will provide children with a variety of practical experiences, and work with the system of numbers 1, 2, 3, . . . can be extracted from these. Later, we can extend these experiences to longer distances and larger units using contrived situations, perhaps, but we must first ensure that children have a working knowledge of the units with which they are dealing and the instruments they are using for measuring, that they can distinguish between a *count* (pure number) and a *measurement*, and can choose the appropriate units for the different ranges of measure.

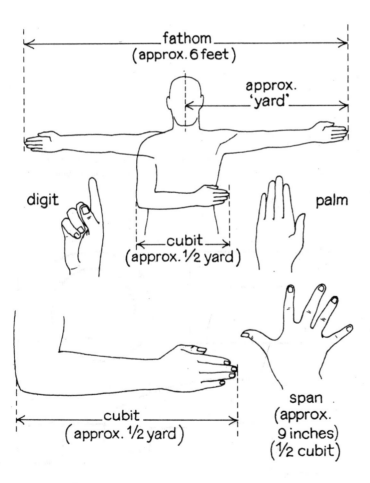

fathom
(approx. 6 feet)

approx.
'yard'

digit

palm

cubit
(approx. ½ yard)

cubit
(approx. ½ yard)

span
(approx.
9 inches)
(½ cubit)

Length

It is interesting to note that, historically, the earliest measurements were calculated from parts of the human body: limb measurements. Many women measure yards of cloth by stretching the material from the tip of their nose to the end of the middle finger of the outstretched arm. A man's 'pace' is roughly one yard in length, and of course the word 'foot' speaks for itself.

This use of the body as a common measure was an important step forward in the history of measurement and it has its origin in visual perception. Therefore, when a child, too, sees an object for measurement he will match it with something he knows: his hand or arm.

When metric units are in use the rough equivalents in metres and centimetres to these limb measurements will have to be discovered by the children.

When children have been brought to realise how inadequate improvised measurements usually are, they will then be ready for work with standard units. It is strongly recommended that lengths of wood or hardboard, or the attractive commercially produced rulers (without end-pieces or sub-divisions) be obtained. The children can be given these to use for measuring tasks to be carried out within or outside the classroom and school; lengths should be recorded in whole yards and whole feet (after estimation) or in metres and decimetres. Measurements of lengths drawn on the blackboard or on the floor, or paper pinned to the wall, and containing an approximate number of units, can be included in the assignments. Perhaps the most fascinating measuring instrument to young children is the trundle- or click-wheel. This has a circumference of one yard or one metre and the wheel clicks each time this measurement is made. For measuring playground and curved lengths, the trundle-wheel is invaluable.

After practical work using yards, metres and decimetres, children can be asked to complete tables as suggested below:

yd	ft
1	3
2	6
3	9
4	.....
5	.....
6	.....
7	.....
8	.....
9	.....
10	.....
.....	33
.....	36
.....	39
.....	42
.....	45

Complete this table.

Can you explain what you were doing?

Can you use this table to change yards to feet or feet to yards?

It is at this stage that we have passed from the real world of measurement back to the set of counting numbers. Although the above table is headed with measuring units, it is essentially the set of the ordered pairs of numbers (1, 3), (2, 6), (3, 9), . . . , the relation being that in each case the second number is three times the first. The table can be built up by successive 'counting on' in threes. The metre table will of course produce the ordered pairs of numbers (1, 10), (2, 20), (3, 30), ...

These relationships are abstracted from the experiences of measuring. It must be emphasised that when we are using the natural numbers, in talking, say, about '6ft', we are using a *mathematical model* or *image* of the far more complicated real world. We can talk of '6ft', but no-one can *exactly* measure 6ft.

When we measure length or height we are really matching the object in question against a standard unit and this enables us to say 'as long as . . . units (imperial or metric)'. In fact, when a child measures the length of an object with his ruler and then draws a line to represent that length he is really matching twice (ruler to object, length of line to ruler).

When experiments by Piaget were carried out with young children it was observed that even though the children seemed to appreciate the conservation of length when objects to be measured were placed in a straight line, when the objects were rearranged in curved or zig zag lines, some children were not so certain. With young juniors, therefore, we give many experiences of curved, round, and zig zag measurements. Here the child will need a pliable measuring tool, a piece of string to match against his ruler, or a tape-measure marked in yards and inches or metres and centimetres.

Calipers can be introduced to children at this stage for measuring diameters of tin lids, balls and cylinders; alternatively these objects can be placed between two blocks.

Suggestions for practical work

Get a large piece of paper and draw lines shaped like these, much bigger of course, using a felt pen or chalk. When you have done this, measure them. Think how you are going to do this, and do not forget to estimate first.

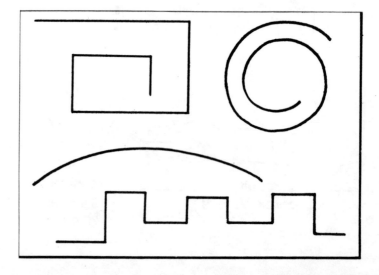

What is the length of your foot?

Draw round it on a piece of paper like this:

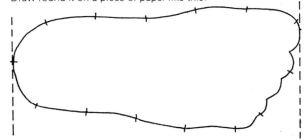

Draw round some other children's feet. Try to find the longest and shortest in the class.

Now, if a man's foot is a foot long, approximately, how much shorter is yours?

How much shorter than a man's foot is the length of the longest foot in the class?

How much shorter is the length of the shortest foot in the class?

What is the distance all the way round your foot? Compare this with your partner's foot.

Do three of your foot-lengths come to about the same as one of your strides?

Draw curved, round or zig zag lines which you think are approximately 10 cm long.

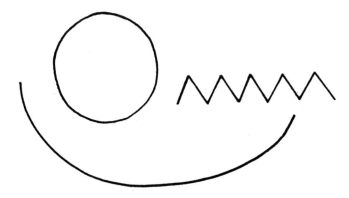

How are you going to check these?

Draw any lines which you think are about 30 cm in length. Check them.

Find as many round objects as you can and see if you can measure the distance round them to the nearest inch (tins and tin lids, balls and buckets—top and bottom).

Make a list of these and record your measurements against each. Don't forget to have a good guess first.

Can you measure the longest distance across the circular shapes?

How will you do this?

Get the calipers and see if you can find out how to use them and find this measurement. which is called the *diameter*.

In using the various standard units of measurement required, the children will no doubt ultimately arrive at fractional parts, when they feel they want to be even more precise with their measuring. We can now introduce the foot rulers with sub-divisions of half and quarter-inches and decimetre rods with sub-divisions of tenths. Halves and quarters are contained in a child's vocabulary almost as soon as he begins to use other names: half a piece of chocolate, a quarter pound of sweets, half-past four, etc. These may be merely words to the child, so far, but, from actual measuring (and the use of money), he can begin to appreciate the meaning of a fractional part, even a tenth.

When dealing with measurements, particularly in metric units, we shall as soon as possible use decimals, so that we can show clearly the degree of accuracy to which we are working.

> Get the cards marked P1 to P6.
>
> Measure the distance all the way round the edges. This is called the *perimeter*. Have a good guess first to the nearest inch. Record your measurements, to the nearest half-inch, and then answer this question:
> Which has the longest perimeter?

Suitable 'shapes' in the above assignment might be: .

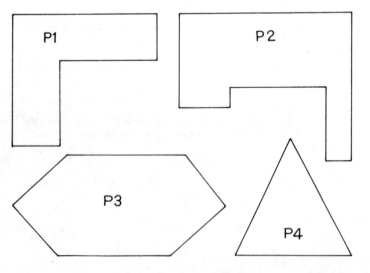

Weight

When the need has been felt for standard weights it is a good idea to begin with the 1lb weight since it is the basic standard unit of a common system of 'weights'. Where metric units of weight have been established the kilogramme or half-kilo could replace the pound. Children can be given assignments which will familiarise them with this unit:

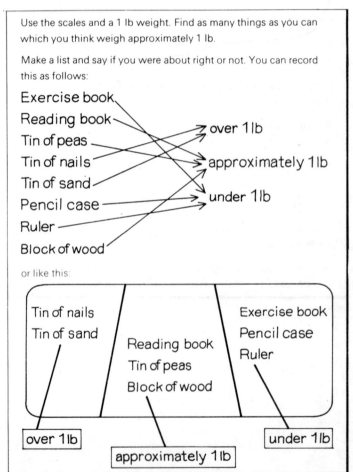

Here we have taken a set of objects, {exercise book, reading book, tin of peas, tin of nails, tin of sand, pencil case, ruler, block of wood}, and partitioned it into three sub-sets, 'over 1lb', 'approximately 1lb in weight' and one having elements 'under 1lb'.

Vincent Keirle   Age 8 yrs.

Estimation

	Estimate	Measure	Error
The door	8 ft	8 ft 9 ins	9 ins.
My height	4 ft	4 ft 4 in	4 in.
My teacher's height	5 ft 11 ins	5 ft 5 ins	6 ins
My stride	2 ft 6 ins	1 ft 9 ins	9 ins
My book	7 ins	8 ins	1 in
A picture	1 ft	1 ft.	0
The blackboard	1 yd	2 ft 11 ins	1 in.
A penny	1 in	1¼ ins	¼ in
Distance round a ball	5 in	7½ ins	2½ ins

I used a piece of string to
go round the ball and then
measured it against my ruler.

This sorting procedure leads us to the relation 'is in the same category as,' which is an equivalence relation since it has the three properties:

i Reflexive

The reading book is in the same weight category as itself (i.e. 'approximately 1lb in weight').

ii Symmetric

If we know that reading book is in the same category as tin of peas, then we know that tin of peas is in the same category as reading book.

iii Transitive

If we know that reading book is in the same category as tin of peas and also that tin of peas is in the same category as block of wood, then we know that reading book is in the same category as block of wood.

But we must specify more carefully what is meant by 'approximately 1lb in weight', in the sense that they are both within one ounce, say, of one pound; they are not necessarily within one ounce of each other. The partition here is '15 oz or less', 'between 15 and 17 oz', '17 oz or more'. The need for ounces has already arisen.

The phrase 'weighs approximately the same as' is usually used differently: for instance, we could use it to mean that two objects differ in weight by less than one ounce. Now this is not an equivalence relation since it fails to satisfy the three properties. We must not infer from

a a penny ($\frac{1}{2}$oz) weighs approximately the same as these sweets (1oz), and

b these sweets weigh approximately the same as an ink bottle (1$\frac{3}{4}$oz) that

c a penny weighs approximately the same as an ink bottle, for the difference in weight between the penny and the ink bottle is more than one ounce. If we were silly enough to do this, we might just as well go on and on, choosing objects such that each was less than one ounce heavier than the previous one, and eventually misuse the transitive property to obtain 'a penny weighs approximately the same as an elephant'.

Children need to see for themselves that 16 of the ounces they have weighed out just about balance 1lb, depending upon the accuracy of the apparatus. Then, having discussed this, we can abstract the mathematical correspondence

lb	oz
1	16
2	32
—	—

When introducing children to the fractional parts of the pound weight it is best that they should be allowed to discover for themselves the relationship between these and ounces. These facts can be recorded in their 'Weight Book'. Useful assignments using the 2oz, $\frac{1}{4}$lb and $\frac{1}{2}$lb weights, etc., can then follow.

You will need the following set of weights: 1 lb, 8 oz, 4 oz, 2 oz, 1 oz. Put these weights in order of size beginning with the heaviest on the left, i.e.

Make a drawing like this in your 'Weight Book'.
Underneath each, write the number of ounces in each weight.
Answer these questions:

1. How many 1 oz weights balance the 2 oz weight?

2. How many 2 oz weights balance the 4 oz weight?

3. How many 4 oz weights balance the 8 oz weight?

4. How many 8 oz weights balance the 1 lb weight?

Do you think you could make some $\frac{1}{2}$ oz and $\frac{1}{4}$ oz 'weights' out of Plasticine, using only the scales and 1 oz 'weights' to help you?

Teachers will see that here is an example of the binary scale:

(1 lb)	(½ lb)	(¼ lb)	(2 oz)	(1 oz)
16	8	4	2	1
2^4	2^3	2^2	2^1	

(It will be recalled that
2^1 means 2
2^2 means 2 x 2
2^3 means 2 x 2 x 2
2^4 means 2 x 2 x 2 x 2).

Some interesting recording using binary notation can be carried out as follows:

Make up some parcels, each weighing a number of ounces or 1lb and a number of ounces. Ask the children to weigh the parcels and record the number of weights used, e.g.

	(1lb)	(8oz)	(4oz)	(2oz)	(1oz)	
Parcel A (2oz)				1	0	(I used one 2oz weight)
Parcel B (4oz)			1	0	0	(I used one 4oz weight)
Parcel C (8oz)		1	0	0	0	and so on
Parcel D (12oz)		1	1	0	0	
Parcel E (20oz)	1	0	1	0	0	

Complete the following table:

Weight in lb	Weight in oz	
1	16	When the teacher has checked this with you, make a graph to show the relationship.
2	..	
3	..	
..	64	
..	80	

A further useful experience for children is to use the spring balance. Elastic bands or springs—they should be fairly strong ones—can be calibrated by hanging the spring or elastic band over a nail fixed in the wall. To the lower end can be attached various weights. If a piece of white card is placed behind the spring, its position, when stretched by a particular weight, can be marked.

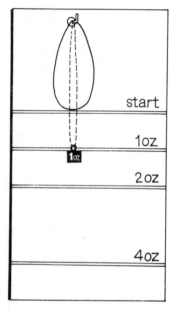

A graph can be plotted from the children's discoveries, using strips of gummed paper to mark the length of stretch. This paper length can then be transferred direct to the graph.

The calibration could show, alternatively, metric units, say 30, 60, 90 grammes. The tiny gramme weight should be available for children to see and feel but the 10-gramme weight is the smallest they can use for actual weighing. The kilogramme should become familiar but it is too large for many classroom purposes. The half-kilo is more useful. But at this stage in children's understanding of number the use of hundred-gramme weights and the reading of such weights as 382 grammes on tins can give meaning to these larger numbers.

Capacity

The children have answered the question 'How much?' in cupfuls, jugfuls, and spoonfuls. We can now proceed to obtain familiarity with vessels holding a pint, $\frac{1}{2}$ pint, quart, and gallon. Cans, bottles, buckets and jugs can now be filled using the standard measures. The only convincing way to show what a bucket holds is to let the child fill it and record the result for himself. Though quarts are seldom used these days it is valuable to let children discover that a quart is a quarter of 1 gallon.

You will need the set of liquid measures:
1 gallon, $\frac{1}{2}$ gallon, quart, pint, $\frac{1}{2}$ pint, gill.
Arrange these measures in order of size, starting with the smallest:
Write them down.

Estimate first, then record:
How many pints can I pour into 1 quart?

How many pints can I pour into 1 gallon?

How many quarts can I pour into 1 gallon?

How many $\frac{1}{2}$ pints can I pour into 1 quart?

How many $\frac{1}{2}$ pints can I pour into 1 gallon?

How many gills can I pour into 1 pint?

How do you think the quart got its name?

If you pour 3 pints into the gallon measure, how many more pints would you need to fill it?

Can you write out a table for these measures?

Write down, in your 'Capacity Book', all those things which you know are usually sold in *pints* or *gallons*, e.g.

Pints	Gallons
Milk	Petrol

There are some 'dry' things as well, which are sold in pints.

Weight Scale

AMOUNT TO BE USED	WEIGHTS USED					
	2 lb	1 lb	8 oz	4 oz	2 oz	1 oz
1 oz						1
2 oz					1	
3 oz					1	1
4 oz				1		
5 oz				1		1
6 oz				1	1	
7 oz				1	1	1
8 oz			1			
9 oz			1			1
10 oz			1		1	
11 oz			1		1	1
12 oz			1	1		
13 oz			1	1		1
14 oz			1	1	1	
15 oz			1	1	1	1
1 lb 0 oz		1				
1 lb 1 oz		1				1
1 lb 2 oz		1			1	
1 lb 3 oz		1			1	1
1 lb 4 oz		1		1		
1 lb 5 oz		1		1		1
1 lb 6 oz		1		1	1	
1 lb 7 oz		1		1	1	1
1 lb 8 oz		1	1			
1 lb 9 oz		1	1			1
1 lb 10 oz		1	1		1	
1 lb 11 oz		1	1		1	1
1 lb 12 oz		1	1	1		
1 lb 13 oz		1	1	1		1
1 lb 14 oz		1	1	1	1	
1 lb 15 oz		1	1	1	1	1
2 lb 0 oz	1					

Doubling and halving are again apparent in our tables of measures.

Children can arrange the measures in order and record them so that this progression becomes more obvious:

gill	$\frac{1}{2}$ pint	1 pint	1 quart	$\frac{1}{2}$ gallon	1 gallon
$\frac{1}{4}$	$\frac{1}{2}$	1	2	4	8

This can be compared with the table of weights on p. 109.

We can help children's awareness of certain relationships through these examples. For instance, they can 'build' tables by counting on in 2s, 4s, and 8s.

gal:	1	2	3	4	5	6 . . .
qt:	4	8	12	16	20	24 . . .

qt:	1	2	3	4	5	6 . . .
pt:	2	4	6	8	10	12 . . .

gal:	1	2	3	4	5	6 . . .
pt:	8	16	24	32	40	48 . . .

The litre, with its sub-unit the millilitre, is the standard metric measure of capacity. Children who have handled a cube with edges of 10 centimetres will quickly learn that an open cube of that size holds, theoretically, 1 litre, and that, corresponding to this, a cube with 1-cm edges holds a thousandth part of a litre, called a millilitre. Chemists in the United Kingdom now issue a millilitre spoon with medicines that have to be measured out.

Work in hundreds and thousands will obviously be involved when children find the capacity, in metric measures, of bottles, jugs, bowls, etc.

It is interesting for children to match the binary pattern (successive doubling) in gallons, quarts and pints with the denary (tens) pattern of the metric units.

ones	10s	100s	litres
1	10^1	10^2	10^3 millilitres

3 Operations and relationships

The four operations are very closely linked: subtraction is the inverse of addition; division the inverse of multiplication. In the early stages, children 'subtract' by adding on and before they can multiply they employ successive addition; for division they keep on 'taking away'. This is all part of their experiences and it is artificial to start with one operation and follow with the others in a particular order. However, when we come to developing the structure of mathematics we shall start with the usual 'addition' operation.

The aim in this section is to give some ideas on number work: pattern, relationships, operations, and properties. Through practical experiences in real situations, using weights and measures, pictorial representations and shapes, children will gradually abstract the underlying structure and patterns of the numbers.

Counting on and back. Use of the number-strip

In order to carry out computation in an efficient manner, children must be able to 'count on', not just in ones, but in 10s, 2s, 5s, 9s, etc. We can lead children to this next stage of development by representing the set of natural numbers (counting numbers) on a number-strip, very much like the number ladder (cf. p. 36).

Many teachers fix a 'master-strip' on the classroom wall (at a convenient height for children) usually marked from 1 to 100. This is made from thin card and given a suitable protective covering of plastic tape or varnish. Smaller strips, representing numbers 1 to 10, are placed in a pocket or hung close to the 'master strip'.

Children can make their own strips from one-inch graph paper stuck on to thin card. At first, a strip representing the set of numbers 1 to 20 can be used, then 20 to 40, 40 to 60, etc., can be added as required. Separate strips representing each number from 1 to 10 will probably be used for carrying out operations in the initial stages.

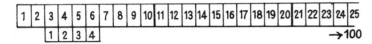

Using the strip children can be asked to count in twos, threes, etc., and, of course, tens. This can be useful preparation not only for 'addition facts' but multiplication as well. Successive addition of the starting number will encourage the memorisation of tables when we wish to do this at a later stage, e.g.,

2, 4, 6, 8, 10, 12, . . . ;
3, 6, 9, 12, 15, 18, . . . ;
4, 8, 12, 16, 20, 24, . . . ;

but other series should be built up also:

1, 3, 5, 7, 9, . . . ;
2, 5, 8, 11, 14, . . . ;
13, 23, 33, 43, 53, . . . ;

Counting backwards is also useful practice for subtraction and division:

15, 12, 9, 6, 3 ;
50, 40, 30, 20, 10 ;
25, 20, 15, 10, 5.

Multiplication and division arise from such questions as

> What number do you reach if you step off the 5-strip along the 'master-strip' four times?
> How many 8-strips are needed to reach 24 ?

In many ways the number-strip serves the same purposes as the 'number-track' of the Stern apparatus. It can give children a visual representation of moves and their patterns so that they achieve an awareness of relationships.

It is not necessary, of course, for the children to record all the moves on the number-strip; in fact they should have times when they are left alone to make their own discoveries at will. It must be remembered that our aim is to eliminate the need for 'counting on' in ones and to familiarise the child with number series as a basis for future operational experiences.

Practical work related to table facts

If we ask the question 'How many wheels on the eight Dinky cars?' we may find that a child will count in ones, but we must grasp the opportunity to lead him to count in fours.

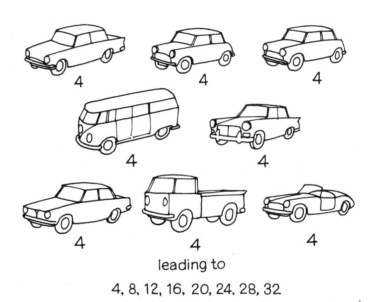

leading to

4, 8, 12, 16, 20, 24, 28, 32

Such activities are beneficial long before we ask the child to memorise tables. By the time we arrive at this stage, if adequate experiences have been encountered and number series have been met in all kinds of situations, most children will have built a good deal into their memory-store and will have considerably improved their chances of 'learning tables'.

Here are other suggestions:

twos: pairs of objects, wholes and halves
threes: length ; sides of sets of triangles
fours: perimeters of squares increasing sides by one unit at a time ; chairs and legs ; animals and legs ; wholes and quarters.
fives: clocks (5-minute intervals) ; fingers and toes
sixes: packing in sixes
sevens: calendar (days in a week)
eights: parts of folded circles, squares, etc.
nines: square pattern of nines, one less than 10
tens: metric measures and decimal coins.

Linda Tyson

0	1	2	3	4	5	6	7	8	9	10	11	12
1	2	3	4	5	6	7	8	9	10	11	12	13
2	3	4	5	6	7	8	9	10	11	12	13	14
3	4	5	6	7	8	9	10	11	12	13	14	15
4	5	6	7	8	9	10	11	12	13	14	15	16
5	6	7	8	9	10	11	12	13	14	15	16	17
6	7	8	9	10	11	12	13	14	15	16	17	18
7	8	9	10	11	12	13	14	15	16	17	18	19
8	9	10	11	12	13	14	15	16	17	18	19	20
9	10	11	12	13	14	15	16	17	18	19	20	21
10	11	12	13	14	15	16	17	18	19	20	21	22
11	12	13	14	15	16	17	18	19	20	21	22	23
12	13	14	15	16	17	18	19	20	21	22	23	24

1.
2.
3
4
5.
6.

using these strips

I made some sums.

3 + 6 = 9   5 + 17 = 22   1 + 8 = 9.

6 + 15 = 21.   4 + 13 = 17.   6 + 13 = 19

5 + 11 = 16.   2 + 14 = 16.   4 + 13 = 17.

The '100' square

At all times we should try to provide a variety of experiences in our number work so that patterns and relationships are seen in many situations. We do not want children always to be thinking of number in terms of length or on a horizontal strip.

The '100' square can be a useful aid to children for observing the patterns which are made by numbers. They enjoy colouring certain numbers and seeing a pattern emerge. This gives a visual image of what could be most abstract.

1	2	3	4	5	6	7	8	9	10
11	12	13	14	15	16	17	18	19	20
21	22	23	24	25	26	27	28	29	30
31	32	33	34	35	36	37	38	39	40
41	42	43	44	45	46	47	48	49	50
51	52	53	54	55	56	57	58	59	60
61	62	63	64	65	66	67	68	69	70
71	72	73	74	75	76	77	78	79	80
81	82	83	84	85	86	87	88	89	90
91	92	93	94	95	96	97	98	99	100

100 square

Children can be asked 'What is the interval between numbers in the vertical columns or on diagonal lines?'

'100' squares can be numbered in a different way and numbers omitted for children to fill in.

100	90	80	70	60	50	40	30	20	10
	89	79	69	59	49	39	29	19	9
98		78	68	58	48	38	28	18	8
97	87		67	57	47	37	27	17	7
96	86	76		56	46	36	26	16	6
95	85	75	65	55	45	35	25	15	5
94	84	74	64	54		34	24	14	4
93	83	73	63	53	43		23	13	3
92	82	72	62	52	42	32		12	2
91	81	71	61	51	41	31	21		1

Many teachers are already finding types of structural apparatus useful in building up patterns of number.

Other useful practice in organising numbers can be obtained from:
numbers on tickets
pages and chapters of a book
numbering a plan of seats for a concert.

6

1	2	3	4	5	6	7	8	9	10
11	12	13	14	15	16	17	18	19	20
21	22	23	24	25	26	27	28	29	30
31	32	33	34	35	36	37	38	39	40
41	42	43	44	45	46	47	48	49	50
51	52	53	54	55	56	57	58	59	60
61	62	63	64	65	66	67	68	69	70
71	72	73	74	75	76	77	78	79	80
81	82	83	84	85	86	87	88	89	90
91	92	93	94	95	96	97	98	99	100

9

1	2	3	4	5	6	7	8	9	10
11	12	13	14	15	16	17	18	19	20
21	22	23	24	25	26	27	28	29	30
31	32	33	34	35	36	37	38	39	40
41	42	43	44	45	46	47	48	49	50
51	52	53	54	55	56	57	58	59	60
61	62	63	64	65	66	67	68	69	70
71	72	73	74	75	76	77	78	79	80
81	82	83	84	85	86	87	88	89	90
91	92	93	94	95	96	97	98	99	100

1

12

1	2	3	4	5	6	7	8	9	10
11	12	13	14	15	16	17	18	19	20
21	22	23	24	25	26	27	28	29	30
31	32	33	34	35	36	37	38	39	40
41	42	43	44	45	46	47	48	49	50
51	52	53	54	55	56	57	58	59	60
61	62	63	64	65	66	67	68	69	70
71	72	73	74	75	76	77	78	79	80
81	82	83	84	85	86	87	88	89	90
91	92	93	94	95	96	97	98	99	100

1

11

1	2	3	4	5	6	7	8	9	10
11	12	13	14	15	16	17	18	19	20
21	22	23	24	25	26	27	28	29	30
31	32	33	34	35	36	37	38	39	40
41	42	43	44	45	46	47	48	49	50
51	52	53	54	55	56	57	58	59	60
61	62	63	64	65	66	67	68	69	70
71	72	73	74	75	76	77	78	79	80
81	82	83	84	85	86	87	88	89	90
91	92	93	94	95	96	97	98	99	100

Kathleen Harrison   Age 9
Adding Square

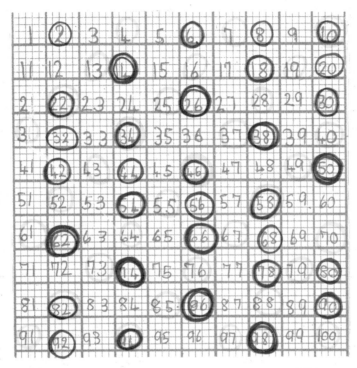

This square is very interesting. It shows that every number which has a red ring round it is every sixth number starting from two instead of nothing. As well as that the numbers which have purple rings round them are every fourth number starting from six. Also each number that has a yellow ring round it is counting in three's starting from number four.

The operation of addition

Young children receive first-hand experience of addition at the classroom shop.

When buying three articles, for example, it may be discovered that
$2 + 3 = 5$
so $(2 + 3) + 7 = 5 + 7 = 12$,
the brackets being used to show that we first find $(2 + 3)$, namely 5, and then $(5 + 7)$, namely 12. But also
$3 + 7 = 10$
so $2 + (3 + 7) = 2 + 10 = 12$
and so $(2 + 3) + 7 = 2 + (3 + 7)$.

This illustrates the *associative* property of the numbers we are considering: $(a + b) + c = a + (b + c)$.

Having made the discovery that $(2 + 3) + 7 = 2 + (3 + 7)$, it is permissible to drop the brackets and write $2 + 3 + 7$, the understanding being that it does not matter in which order the operations are carried out.

A set of objects can be partitioned in different ways, and the children can be asked to record their various rearrangements in terms of the numbers of elements of the sub-sets, e.g.

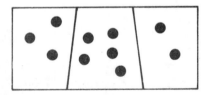

Partitioning in other ways, $8 + 2 = 10$, etc.

Children have already seen that addition is *commutative*, i.e. the order of the numbers does not matter. For example,
$6 + 4 = 4 + 6$
(see p. 50).

Using both the commutative and the associative properties, we can add in any order we wish. For example, to add
$6 + 7 + 2 + 3 + 4$,
we can write
$(6 + 4) + (7 + 3) + 2$
$= 10 + 10 + 2$
$= 22$.

'Addition facts' or 'bonds' are still important but these should not be approached in a dreary or monotonous way but as patterns.

Children can be led to observe symmetrical patterns, and the role of zero can again be pointed out, though it should not be laboured as it has been in the past.

The symmetrical patterns can be shown in tables or squares such as the following:

+	0	1	2	3	4
0	0	1	2	3	4
1	1	(2)	3	4	5
2	2	3	(4)	5	6
3	3	4	5	(6)	7
4	4	5	6	7	(8)

i The commutative property, e.g. $2 + 3 = 3 + 2$.
ii The 'doubled' numbers which appear on the diagonal from upper left to lower right

$1 + 1$ (2)
$2 + 2$ (4)
$3 + 3$ (6)
$4 + 4$ (8)

Children can be asked to find a number which when added to another number gives a sum in the body of the table square, e.g.

'What number must be added to 3 to give 7 ?'

This question can be asked in the form:
3 + ☐ = 7. What number must be put in the box to make this a true statement?

From their 'counting on' experiences, children have little difficulty with examples such as 6 + 4 = ☐. The real problems are contained in the following situations:

6 + ☐ = 10,
☐ + 5 = 8,
☐ + 3 = △ + 2

Each of these is an 'open sentence'. The problem is to find numbers to put in the ☐ or △ in order to make the sentence *true*. In the first example, the required number is 4; in the last, we can find many pairs of numbers, for example 5 in ☐ and 6 in △. In fact a table could be made:

■	▲
5	6
6	7
2	3
0	1
7	8

etc.

4   Place value

From their experiences with number-strips and other equipment and the study of other notations, children have been receiving an informal introduction to our system of place value. There is, however, still a danger of underestimating the difficulties which this presents to children. Teachers know what pitfalls are created by 0; in the past even older children have been confused over the values of each numeral contained in a given number (e.g. what does the '5' represent in 256?). This is probably due to the fact that many of them had never seen a practical representation of the position and consequent value of a numeral in our system of notation.

A variety of structural apparatus is helpful at this stage in establishing the notion of place value. Some children will take more readily to one piece of apparatus than another (and so a variety should be available) and some will quickly get the successive ideas and not need so much practical experience.

The use of different 'number bases' focuses attention on place value in its own right without being tied to the customary 'base ten'. When we write 37 this means (by convention)
3 tens and 7 units,
which could be written
3(10) + 7.

Reference should, however, be made to p. 109 where the weight of parcel A is recorded as 10 since it balanced with 1 two-oz weight and 0 one-oz weights.

Instead of 10 meaning
1 *ten* and 0 units,
in the 'scale of two' (or 'binary' scale), 10 means
1 *two* and 0 units.

The base is *two* instead of *ten*.

The Dienes multi-base arithmetic blocks give structural experience with different bases (up to ten). The material is so designed that the children build according to the base they are using. At first, it is recommended that children play with the material until they discover the relationships between the pieces.

As an example, these are the standard pieces in base three.

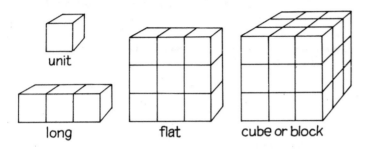

unit

long　　　　　flat　　　　cube or block

Children will probably start just playing with them, making towers, houses, aeroplanes, . . . and this phase must not be hurried. The children will later discover that three 'units' match against a 'long'

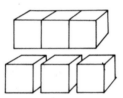

and then start making exchanges (3 units for a long, 3 longs for a flat and so on). They can actually see that 3 units can be traded for 1 long; or, given 7 units that 6 of them can be traded for 2 longs (of 3 units each).

longs	units
	□ □ □
	□ □ □
	□

6 can be traded for 2 longs.

longs	units
□□□	□
□□□	

This is a first step towards realising that, for example, 17 units (in conventional base 10) can be replaced by
1 ten and 7 units
and that this is what we mean when we write '17'. Children should get used to working in different bases on different occasions, and the teacher should provide the opportunity for them to change over frequently, the '10-box' (leading to our 'usual' notation) happening to be one of them.

Various forms of abacus are useful in the same connection, though it is more sophisticated to exchange, say, 3 washers on one peg for a similar washer *of the same size* on the next.

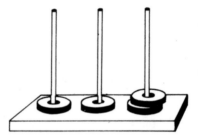

Abacus consisting of wooden pegs (or meat skewers mounted on Plasticine) and plastic washers.

Here, for example, having agreed to be using 'base 3', a washer on the right counts as a unit, one in the middle as 3 and a left-hand one as 3^2 (i.e. 9). The abacus in the diagram represents 14, ($3^2 + 3 + 2$).

Another variation is the 'counting board' here shown with base 4, but the set of numbers at the top can be changed according to the base used.

64	16	4	1
	●	● ● ●	● ●

This could be home-made using small plastic tablets, buttons, shells, etc., as counters.

All sorts of other aids can be used. One of the simplest is bundles of sticks, matchsticks, spills, straws, or pen-handles. These can be tied in bundles of ten.

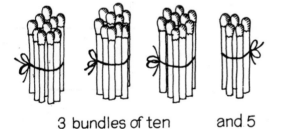

3 bundles of ten   and 5   total 35

Part V
Shape and size

The further experience of shape and size outlined in this section builds on the activities suggested in Parts II and III.

Geometry is sometimes thought of as investigation or discovery of pattern and relationship in shape, size and place. These are observed in, and derived from, the immediate environment and the much wider world, both natural and man-made.

Mathematics is very much concerned with relationships. A relation makes no sense on its own; examples have been given such as *belongs to, was born in the month of*. Relationships exist between members or 'elements' of sets. Spatial relationships can be considered in a similar way. Suppose Johnny breaks a window at school. As a temporary repair the caretaker fits a piece of cardboard into the window shape.

We have:

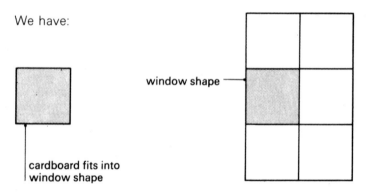

cardboard fits into window shape

window shape

The cardboard *fits into* the window shape.

Fits into is the relationship between the two shapes. The cardboard fits because its sides and angles correspond to those of the window shape.

Later on, the glazier uses the same relationship when he fits a new piece of glass. Then the window cleaner arrives. He props his ladder against the wall.

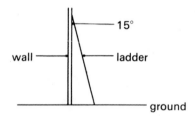

wall · ladder · 15° · ground

The ladder *is at an angle to* the wall. *Is at an angle to* is the relation. If the angle can be measured the relationship can be stated as 'the ladder makes an angle of 15° with the wall'.

Photographs can be obtained as enlargements of the originals. Later we shall see that there is a relationship in this. The enlargement *is similar to* the original photograph.

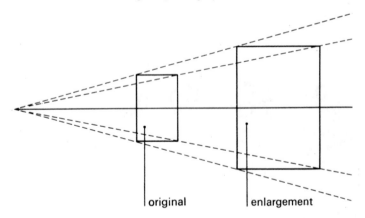

original · enlargement

This idea also occurs with three-dimensional shapes. Dinky toys and model aircraft, for instance, are scale models of the real things.

These are but a few of the many relationships which will be investigated in work on shape and size.

The idea of a set can be used to advantage in our study of spatial relationships.

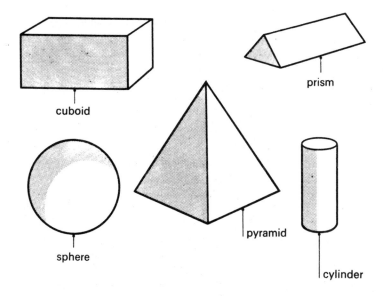

cuboid

prism

sphere

pyramid

cylinder

Having looked at 'relationships' in this general way we can now consider the approach to geometry in the primary school. It can be thought of as concerned with space and shape in the material world, and this world embraces all aspects of a child's life, at home, outside the home and at school. Introducing this idea of geometry will help the child to realise and appreciate that mathematics is something which has grown as man has studied his environment, has tried to describe it and to control it. Geometrical ideas, then, deserve inclusion as just one example of the ubiquity of mathematics.

As a child abstracts the idea of number from his early experiences of collections of things, so his experience of the visible, tangible world of objects will lead to the abstraction of geometrical ideas of shape and size and place. The development of spatial concepts, geometrical ideas — call it what you will — lends itself admirably to discovery, even with the youngest children, and requires little expensive material.

There are three aspects of the 'unity of learning' in which a study of geometry plays its part in the primary school. These can be summarised as the linking of geometry with
a   other aspects of mathematics,
b   other class activities,
c   the rest of the children's lives.

The young child playing with three-dimensional shapes such as cuboids, pyramids, prisms, spheres, cylinders, may find that he can stand his cuboid shapes on top of each other in several ways; that his cylinders can be built up one on top of the other but not as easily as cuboids; that pyramids have a 'point', and so on. In doing this he is beginning to sort or classify. Among the set of geometrical solids he is distinguishing the sub-set of cuboids, the sub-set of cylinders and so on. When he looks at two-dimensional shapes, perhaps those which have been noticed as 'faces' or surfaces of the three-dimensional shapes, he finds squares, rectangles, triangles, circles, etc. Some are four-sided shapes (quadrilaterals), some have three sides (triangles), some are circles. If we think of the set of two-dimensional shapes we have the sub-sets of all quadrilaterals, all triangles, all circles, etc. Again, squares, rectangles, rhombuses and trapezia form sub-sets of the set of quadrilaterals.

a Other aspects of mathematics

Geometrical ideas can establish a link with other aspects of mathematics, and already it has been noted that spatial relationships are some of the many relationships in mathematics which can overlap and make the subject one whole, not a series of isolated branches. We give a few examples.

i Patterns with shapes, squares, rectangles, etc., can lead to number relationships and table building and may involve some computation ; figurate numbers such as
square numbers:

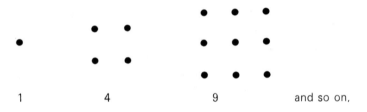

| 1 | 4 | 9 | and so on, |

triangular numbers:

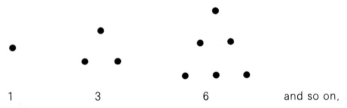

| 1 | 3 | 6 | and so on, |

involve patterns in shape and in number.

ii If a square piece of card is turned about a point at its centre, there are four positions where it appears unchanged, i.e. looks as it did at the start.

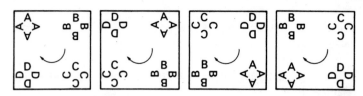

This is an aspect of the *rotational symmetry* of a square. It is a four-fold rotational symmetry. The square card can be turned over and another four positions result. So if we include all the rotations and turning over as well, there are eight positions. This is an eight-fold symmetry.

iii Here we have another link with number.

8	1	6
3	5	7
4	9	2

This is a '1 to 9 magic square'. The horizontal rows, vertical columns, and the two diagonals give the same total, 15. If this square is printed in dots on tracing paper, or thin writing paper, in the pattern shown and on both sides of the paper so that the dots on each side coincide, eight-fold symmetry can be used to show eight possible ways of transforming this square so that it is still 'magic'.

The eight ways are illustrated here :

Starting position.   Turning paper through one right angle about centre each time.

The paper is then turned over and these positions are seen:

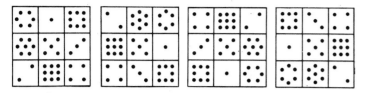

Starting position. Turning paper through one right angle about centre each time.

For example, the last one could be written:

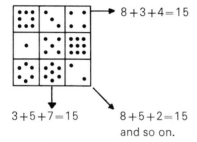

$8+3+4=15$

$3+5+7=15$ $8+5+2=15$ and so on.

In fact this is much more than a link with number, for the unifying power of mathematics is represented by the fact that any one of the eight positions can always be arrived at from any other by just one of the eight rotations of reflections (see p. 127). The 'eight' does not really matter: what matters is the idea that you can always get from some given position to some other given position in just one of a specified series of steps.

iv Many of the relationships can be expressed in graphical form, others can lead to generalisation and perhaps an introduction to algebra; symmetry introduces children to 'motion geometry' and 'groups' which will be developed at the secondary stage.

b Other class activities

In the overall pattern of primary school work, much of the work on shape and size can arise from, or be linked with, other branches of learning. In geography and science, for instance, the compass has its connection with the angle, half right-angle and so on. Movement of the earth in relation to the sun leads to shadow variation and height measurement. Maps and scale drawing can start with the immediate environment, the classroom and its neighbourhood, and be linked with simple surveying. Distances on the globe will introduce ideas such as the great circle.

History may bring in the plumb-line and the 3, 4, 5 rope used by the Egyptians.

Rope knotted into 12 lengths (made as nearly as possible the same).

Rope stretched to give right-angled triangle.

There were early attempts at map making, e.g. in the Domesday Book, and Columbus's voyages, which can link history, geography and work on scales and maps.

Primary school 'geometry' is not concerned with theorems as such, but with pattern and relationships. One theorem, however, that is particularly interesting and useful is that of Pythagoras, which states that 'the square on the hypotenuse is equal to the sum of the squares on the other two sides of a right-angled triangle'.

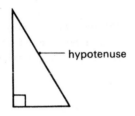
hypotenuse

History and pattern can come together. For many years before Pythagoras lived, mosaic tile patterns in China illustrated his 'theorem'. This can be linked with discoveries on covering surfaces with tiles and different shapes in our primary school work.

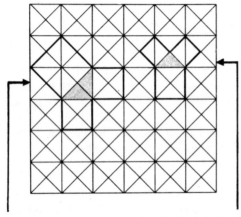

Here the square on the hypotenuse consists of 8 small triangles. On each of the other sides the square consists of 4 small triangles.

For the shaded triangle it can be seen that the square on the hypotenuse is made up of 4 small triangles. The square on each of the other two sides is made up of 2 triangles.

Needlework, too, should not be overlooked, for patterns done by even young children may bring in ideas of symmetry and involve reflection, rotation and translation. (See p. 55.)

Model making, itself a frequent part of history and geography and other environmental studies, will use ideas of scale and similarity. Wigwams for Indian model villages, for instance, might be made from paper cones with the mathematics arising from the discovery of how to get the height and floor size required.

Teachers will constantly find mathematics arising from other work; it cannot be separated from the rest of children's learning.

c   The rest of the children's lives

Here an even broader view is taken. Ideas of shape and size will sometimes arise from things seen and experienced outside the classroom. Alternatively, geometrical ideas may be introduced first and practical examples of them sought. For example, discovery of what shapes occur in a fairground, on railways, in the school, in churches, in games such as hopscotch or football, can lead to consideration of why things are a particular shape. Patterns of rectangular tiles seen on floors can be associated with properties of rectangles, symmetry, parallels and the idea of covering a surface.

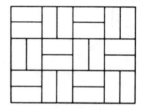 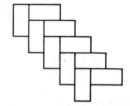

These patterns show that rectangular and square tiles can occupy the same space in several ways, and can cover a surface without gaps. From this it can be sensed that opposite sides are equal, all angles are equal, and the angles are 'right angles'. Again, patterns of regular hexagons may be seen. These will show that regular hexagons can occupy the same space in several ways and can cover a surface without gaps or overlapping. Their angles, however, are not right angles. Also, regular pentagons can occupy the same space in several ways but cannot cover a surface without gaps. This can tell us something about their angles.

Work on 'strong' shapes, such as the triangle and arch, can lead to discovery of examples of their applications outside the school in such things as bridges and cranes.

Summary of aims and approach

The ideas outlined above are a far cry from the formal approach of Euclid with his 'proofs': the children need a lively, dynamic approach. It is worthwhile going right back to the ages before Euclid and looking at some of the beginnings of geometry. When man began to build he became aware of the need for measuring devices other than those for length. This brought the need for right angles; land had to be marked out, areas calculated, heights of buildings worked out, and so on. These showed the importance of shapes such as the square, rectangle, triangle, circle, and what man could do with them. The properties of these shapes became his tools and these properties were found by using them, by action, by discovery. These experiences inevitably led to a discovery of relationships and rules, to the 'laws' of geometry.

Our approach should be 'doing', discovering, building up experience; the manner of approach of the early, practical people gives us a lead.

We can look at geometry in terms of movement or other alteration of shapes rather than through the more static, formal approach of 'proof-seeking'. The mathematician Felix Klein said in 1872 that all geometry could be thought about by moving or changing a geometrical figure and seeing which properties did *not* alter. We can consider changes or transformations such as reflection, rotation, translation and find out which properties do not change. For example, look at the square and the properties which do not change when it undergoes the various transformations shown below.

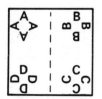
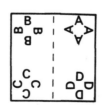

reflection

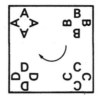
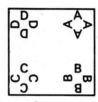

rotation
through a right
angle

or through different angles, e.g.

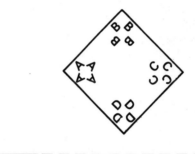

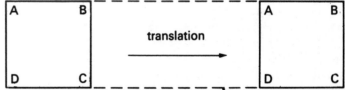

translation

Under each of these transformations, length, for instance, is unchanged, so are angle and area. Other transformations give different results. If we look back at the enlargement on p. 122 we see that it preserves shape, but not area. In the primary school we should provide experiences of moving shapes which bring in elementary ideas of reflection, rotation, translation and enlargement, and thus build up a background for further studies of geometry.

Discovery in the early years is quite informal and springs from immediate experience. Now it is important that there is progression, that the discovery is purposeful, has a meaning and does not just become a random and unrelated activity. If these activities of the children are to be of real benefit, teachers must make themselves familiar with the mathematical ideas and experience them for themselves. Planning and arranging the situations for discovery, taking advantage of interest, are not enough. To see what and how the children are thinking, there must be discussion and talking with them, and this will often involve asking the vital question which starts off a new line of thought.

2   Children's activities

The activities suggested here are set out in such a way as to show progression in each topic, and are intended for small groups of children. A suitable group is three or four children helping each other through discussion among themselves. Frequently there is a 'spiral' treatment of a topic, returning to the subject at different levels of development. The reasons for this are (i) to build on previous experience and thus to amplify and provide progression in understanding, and (ii) to look at something in retrospect. Some point which may not be fully grasped initially will frequently become simplified when tackled at the next stage. And, of course, the children will be older and more mature in appreciation.

It is of great value for children to make up their own assignments and problems for each other to try after having worked through the ideas suggested for their group. Thinking out a problem for someone else involves the imagination and thought not only of the child attempting to solve the problem, but also of the one who has to compile it. Some of the topics will involve looking at things outside the school and associating these with discoveries in the classroom. At times the reverse will apply. For instance, one of the assignments involves fitting blocks and wooden bricks together in the classroom and then finding how this occurs in buildings, floors, and so on. But this could arise the other way. A general study of a building site might lead to discussion on the ways bricks fit together, and in this case the teacher can refer to the suggestions on pp. 134-136 to see where mathematics can be used.

a Filling three-dimensional space
Volume and capacity

As when measuring length children use a variety of materials and methods before meeting standard units, so with three-dimensional shapes they should have plenty of informal activities involving volume. In particular, they should encounter the two aspects of volume (as the amount of space a solid occupies, and as the amount of space in a hollow container, alternatively referred to as capacity) before thinking about measurement in standard units.

Invariance of volume is discussed on p. 17 and as a check that children have understood this, here is a test designed for individuals rather than groups.

It investigates what happens to the volume of a solid shape made of cubes when the cubes are rearranged.

You will need 24 one-inch or one-centimetre cubes.

Ask the child to make two blocks which look the same, each to contain the same number of cubes. How does he know?

Move one set of cubes to make a new shape. Do the two sets still take up the same amount of space?

If he says yes, ask him why he is sure. Answers which indicate the blocks were the same to start with, with the same amount of wood in each (or similar ideas), are satisfactory and show that the child has grasped the concept.

If he says no, then he requires more activities with bricks and blocks, building with the same number and rearranging a number of bricks to make different shapes and so on before he is tested again.

When children seem to have satisfactorily grasped the idea of invariance of volume as the space occupied by three-dimensional shapes, activities such as the following can be introduced to test whether they understand the invariance of the amount of space in a container:

2. Stephen said get some scales that go like this U and put the water in and weigh it. We havent any scales like this.

Steven Johnson

We weighed the jar. It weighed 4 pounds and 4 ounces.

To find out how much the water weighed we took away the weight of the jar from the weight of the jar and water together.

Robert Green.

I said find something that doesnt weigh anything and put the water in it. We couldnt find something that didnt weigh anything.

Frederick Mesher

Michael said "We know how much the jar and water weigh together 9 pounds and 3 ounces (2lb) (2lb) (1lb) (1lb) (1lb) (1lb) (½oz) (½oz) (½oz) (½oz) We didnt have enough weights. We had to borrow a one pound weight from Miss Wildman and a one pound weight from Mrs. Bannerjee.

We took two (2lb) (2lb) weights away for the 4 pounds. (2lb) (2lb) We couldnt take away 4 ounces because there were only 3 ounces there (2oz) (1oz).

Stephen took one (8oz) weight and changed it into two (4oz) weights. Then he took away one (4oz) weight and said that makes 15 ounces left. The answer is 4 lbs 15 ounces.

Miss Branney said If we find out how much the jar weighs - - -

3.

The weight of the jar and the water together.

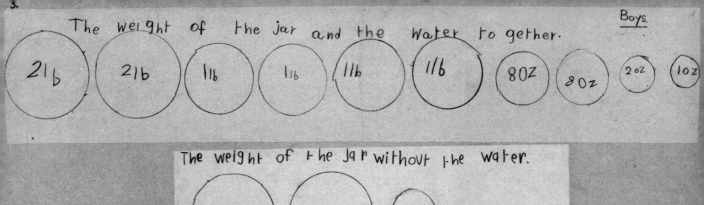

2lb 2lb 1lb 1lb 1lb 1lb 8oz 8oz 2oz 1oz

The weight of the jar without the water.

2lb 2lb 4oz

The weight of the water.

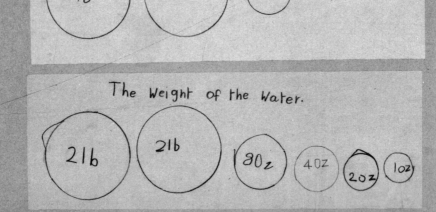

2lb 2lb 8oz 4oz 2oz 1oz

> You will need the chalk box, pen-nib box and some sand.
> Estimate how many small boxfuls of sand will fill the large box.
> Fill the large box with sand by using the small box.
> Count how many small boxes full of sand you used.
> How good was your estimate?
> Was it too many or not enough?

Similar activities can be given using wooden cubes to fill a box, packing small boxes of about the same size into a larger box, and so on.

Other activities:

> Marbles and a jam jar
> How many marbles do you think you will need to fill this jar?
> Try it and see.
> Do you think marbles are very good for finding how much space there is in the jar?
> Why?

Discuss this with children, and ask for suggestions for better material, etc.

> Small balls and a large box
> How many balls do you think you will need to fill this box?
> Try it and see how near you were.

Marbles, cubes, and so on can also be used for packing (or trying to fill) containers such as cylindrical tins.

From these activities teachers can discuss the various things used, e.g., marbles, sand, 1-inch cubes for filling boxes and other containers; pen-nib boxes or match-boxes to measure the sand needed to fill a container. Comparisons can be made – for some three-dimensional shapes, e.g. some of the boxes, 1-inch cubes provide an easy way of measuring the amount of space; for others, it is easier to use a small box to measure sand to fill the container.

Further discussion can bring out the difficulty of comparing the volume (capacity) of containers using these units, etc., as match-boxes, pen-nib boxes, cups, will vary. Can we have something which everyone can use? (Cf. pp. 73–79.)

For packing into some boxes the 1-inch cube is useful. When cubes fit without leaving gaps we can count the number used. The amount of space a 1-inch (or 1-centimetre) cube occupies is 1 cubic inch (or cubic centimetre). We can measure the amount of space in cubic inches by using these cubes. But what about the gaps when cubes do not fit, as in the case of containers such as jars and cylindrical tins? We have seen that these cubes are then not suitable. Small boxes were used to measure the amount of sand to fill the containers; now we can introduce a 'standard' box. Some children may be able to make an open 1-inch cube of stiff cartridge paper or strawboard to use as a 'box' for this purpose. But where difficulty is experienced by young children, it should be made by the teacher. The 1-centimetre cube is too small for young children to make.

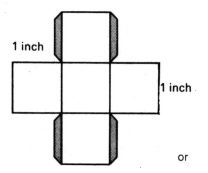

1 inch

1 inch

or

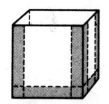

Paper folded and fastened with an adhesive at the flaps.

5 separate 1-inch squares of strawboard fastened with Sellotape.

This 'box' can then be introduced as a measure for filling containers with sand, etc., and the fact that it holds 1 cubic inch discussed. Practice in using this can be given, and children can count the number of cubic inches a container holds. We now have two 'measures', both of which can be used to find volume or

MARBLES AND A JAR

Filling a jar with marbles

We took a one lb jam jar and a box of marbles. Then we guessed how many marbles it would take to fill the jar.

Our Guesses

Name	Number of Marbles
Fiona said	79
(Susan) I said	51
Gillian said	80
Peter said	90

1) We wondered how many marbles there really were in the jar so we filled it full to the top and then counted them. There were 80.

2) We recounted them to check and found that our first answer was correct.

3) Therefore, Gillian's guess was quite correct; Fiona's was only 1 out, Peter guessed 10 too many while I guessed 29 too few. I must try to do better next time.

4) We all think that marbles are not very good for finding how much space there is in the jar because
(Peter) They are round, and leave spaces in between.
(Fiona) They don't go right to the edge of the jar.
(Gillian) They don't fill the jar completely.
  I, Susan Binns, have recorded this.

I, Peter, drew the Marbles.

Our Team
1 Vanda Spencer - Aged 9
2 Jillian Homer - 8
3 Susan Binns - 9
4 Peter Cartlidge 8

SHAPES WE CAN MAKE FROM OUR MODEL

We made a model the
same shape as our chalk
box.
It was 6 cubes long
It was 4 cubes wide
It was 3 cubes high

We used 72 cubes in
our model

Our model took up the
same space as our box
and it had the same
volume.

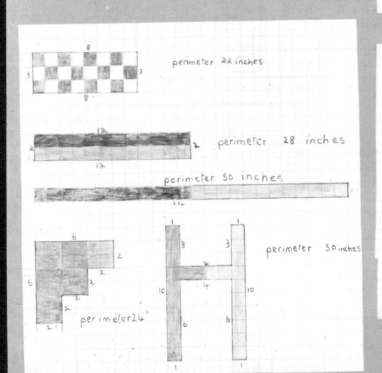

perimeter 22 inches

perimeter 28 inches

perimeter 50 inches

perimeter 50 inches

perimeter 24"

We made all
these shapes
they are all
three blocks
deep

Although we
had the same
number of cubes
in each shape
the length of
the perimeter
is different

If we took a
piece of string
and wrapped
it round we
should use more

string on
some shapes
than others

Class 3B Age 8-9
Karen Hunter Susan Slater
Christopher Potter

capacity: solid 1-inch cubes can be used when they fit suitably, and a 1-inch cube 'box' can be used for filling containers. (Centimetre units can also be used.)

Which shapes fit together best?

This investigation will be considered from several aspects. It provides early experience on which to build ideas of symmetry; it can lead to the discovery of properties of 'regular' shapes, three-dimensional and two-dimensional; it is a preparation for discovery at a much later stage of the generalised way of calculating the volume of cuboids, etc.

A group of children will have, say, twenty-four of each shape of brick or block of a given size (cube, cuboid, prism, cylinder, etc.).

Use all the blocks of one kind.
Try to build a wall which has at least two thicknesses of brick.
Do this with all the shapes. You may put the bricks in any pattern you wish.
Which shapes did you find were the easiest for building walls?
Why do you think this is?

The children should have found that the cube and rectangular shaped bricks were the best. This is because these bricks can occupy the same place in several ways. They have 'square corners' and parallel faces which fit together, and opposite faces of the same shape and size. House bricks, toy building bricks, constructional games use these shapes for this reason. Children will come across many examples, particularly in their toys and games, and so these 'regular' shapes are considered before irregular ones.

The development of this discovery, that cuboid shapes fit together best, will be to find out more about these shapes, and some assignments are given below.

Build a wall two bricks thick using the cubes.
Can you take out any brick, turn it round and replace it in its hole?
See if you can find out how many ways you can replace a brick.
You may mark the faces of the brick if this will help you.

Build a wall two bricks thick using the rectangular bricks.
Find some walls made of bricks — at school or outside the school, and see if you can find out how the bricks are fitted together. (A garden wall may be useful.)
Which do you think gives the strongest wall, one made from cubes or one made from rectangular bricks?
Why?
Can you take out any brick from your wall and turn it round and replace it?
In how many ways can you put it back?
You may mark the face to help you.

At a later stage children may use this work as a link with computation. For instance, if 30 bricks are made into a wall they could be arranged:

5 bricks in a layer of one thickness, with
3 layers and
2 thicknesses.

This leads to the expression $(5 \times 3) \times 2$ for the number of bricks, which indicates a sequence of multiplications.

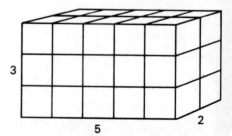

Alternatively, an arrangement of
3 bricks in a layer of one thickness, with
2 layers and
5 thicknesses.

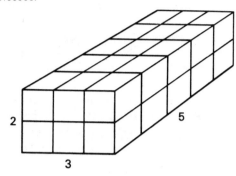

leads to the expression $(3 \times 2) \times 5$ for the number of bricks, and so on.

> Look at your walls. Look at the corners of the bricks.
> Why do you think cubes and rectangular bricks fit together well?
> Look round the school and see if you can find any other examples of these shapes fitted together.
> Now try to write down as many reasons as you can why these shapes are used a lot in building.

The ideas brought out will probably include the facts that there are 'square corners' which fit together well, that the bricks can be replaced easily, that it is easy to make the top of the wall level (linked with parallel lines of mortar, etc.).

The teacher will have to introduce the term 'right angle' for the 'square corner' of rectangular faces, and show the children how to make a 'right-angle tester' by folding a piece of paper twice.

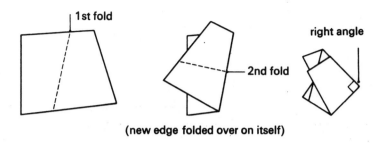

(new edge folded over on itself)

It is interesting to ask the children why we do not use the corner of a sheet of exercise paper. Can they suggest a reason?

> Can you see any more right angles in the classroom? (Or about the school?)
> Test them by fitting your folded-paper right angle onto the shapes.
> Open out your folded paper. How many right angles can you find where the creases cross?

> Do you know how a bricklayer (builder) makes sure the bricks (floor) are level? (Do any children have fathers who are bricklayers?)
> What would happen to this marble if the desk (floor) were not level?
> Try it.
> Make a tester from two rulers and a marble.
> Check the level of surfaces.

A 'level' tester

Two upright rulers with small blocks or cubes at ends. Bind on with Sellotape

Introduce the word 'horizontal' (not only of 'plane' but lines, e.g. mortar lines between bricks, window-frame bars, etc.).
'Can you see any more horizontals in the classroom?
Test with a spirit level.'

What else must a builder check in his building? ('Vertical' may have to be brought out by questioning. Does he want it to lean over?)
Have any children watched Father putting up a post?
How does he get it 'upright'?
Introduce the word 'vertical'.
How do the bricklayer and Father check this? (Plumb-line.)
Make a plumb-line from thin string and a small, heavy weight.
Find some examples of what look like verticals and test them with the plumb-line.

Vertical and horizontal
A jam jar about half full of water is required.

'Stand jar on desk. Does the water surface look horizontal?
(Test with a spirit level held in front of jar.)
Carefully tilt jar one way. Is the surface still horizontal?

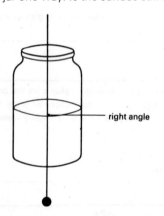

Some teachers may prefer to use a 'jar' with a rectangular base, such as a small fish tank.

right angle

Tilt in some other directions and examine the water level.
Hold plumb-line in front of the jar. Put your eye so that the surface of the top of the water looks like a straight line.
What angles do you see where the plumb-line crosses the line of the water surface?
Can you say what angles you see when a vertical line crosses a horizontal line?'

b From three dimensions to two

Fitting shapes together – Symmetry
The patterns shown by the faces of bricks can now be used to develop the idea of covering a two-dimensional surface. Most of the tiles children see on walls, floors they walk on, paving stones they run and jump on, use rectangular shapes, so the work in the early stages will largely be concerned with these shapes. In any case this is a natural development from three-dimensional bricks.

In this section, when emphasis will be on fitting shapes together (and not on area), we are concerned with discovering that some shapes will fit together without leaving a gap or overlapping. We are not concerned with boundaries, e.g., what happens at the end of the wall or on reaching the edges of the floor.

The children look for patterns in brickwork, tiles and floors.

Most brickwork in houses and other load-bearing walls is arranged so that joins between bricks are not directly one above the other. This is called bonding.

If the wall is only half a brick thick, i.e. $4\frac{1}{2}$ inches, the method is known as *Stretcher Bond.*

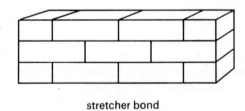

stretcher bond

The commonest ways of fitting bricks together for a wall a brick thick, i.e. 9 inches, are *English Bond* and *Flemish Bond*.

Other suggestions for work

Groups of children can be given tiles made from coloured card, or cut from lino or vinyl floor covering. These can be in squares, rectangles, triangles or 'diamonds'.

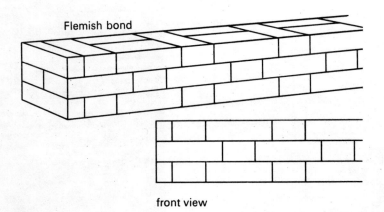

English bond

front view

Flemish bond

front view

> Make tile patterns by fitting these shapes together. See in how many ways you can make a pattern with the rectangles. (Repeat with squares and rectangles used together.)
> Find how many ways you can turn a square round so that it still fits into the pattern. What about a rectangle?
> How much do you have to turn a rectangle so that it fits into its hole in a new position? More than for a square? How much more?

The pattern shown on p. 124 has introduced the first ideas of 'rotational symmetry', which will be studied more fully later on.

The idea of symmetry, or balance, in shapes can now be investigated in other ways. One avenue for exploration is pattern work in art and craft activities. Blot patterns may have been made already and these can be recalled or developed again. Others can be made by paper folding and cutting, pricking, and drawing.

> Take a plain sheet of paper about the size of a page in an exercise book, or slightly larger. Fold it in two. Open out the paper and drop a 'blob' of paint (or ink) on the fold. Now fold your paper again and carefully press it all over. Open it and lay it flat to dry. What do you notice about the shape you have made?
> Tell me about the shapes you can see on each side of the fold. How has this happened?
> Does it look like anything you know?

(It may resemble a leaf, or a butterfly, for instance.)

FLOOR PATTERN

Reproduction of classroom floor pattern made by a nine-year-old girl

FLOOR PATTERN

JAYNE HOWLETT

The following work is by a group of 'below-average' nine-year-olds.

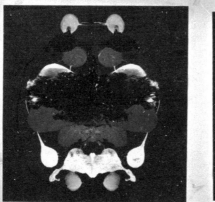
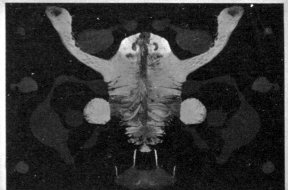

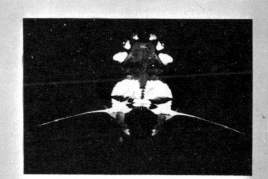
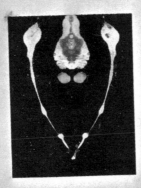

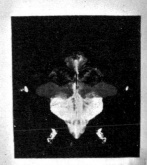

BLOT PATTERNS

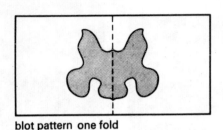

blot pattern one fold

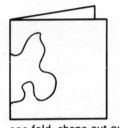

one fold, shape cut out

two resultant shapes from cut-out

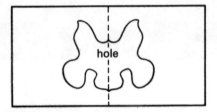

hole

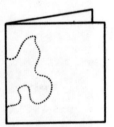

one fold, prick through

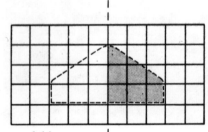

one fold, copy shape on one half on to other half

Interesting shapes can be produced using the experience gained by the children in folding squares and rectangles of paper. These can be folded once, or twice, or more, and shapes cut out after folding. The children can guess what the resultant shape will look like before opening out the paper.

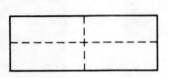

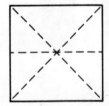

There are many examples of natural shapes which are symmetrical and this is the time to make a collection of these. Children should be encouraged to look for such things as leaves, butterflies, and other shapes which could be 'folded' or cut, in one way, in two ways (for some children even three ways, four ways . . .), so that symmetry can be seen, and to show the 'axes of symmetry'.

More activities with patterns

Many young children enjoy making repeating patterns, such as potato prints or simple needlework patterns, and these may introduce ideas of rotation, reflection, and translation. Much of the work will arise naturally from pattern making in art activities and teachers should discuss the ways in which the patterns have occurred.

At other times, activities involving reflection, rotation and translation in patterns can be suggested.

For instance, when making potato prints it might be suggested that the potato is cut to give a pattern.

such as this  or this

These could be used for patterns showing 'reflection'.

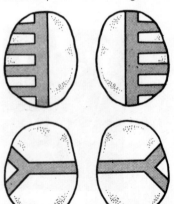

Rotation can be shown thus:

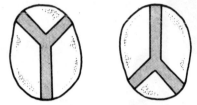

and repeating a pattern can introduce translation:

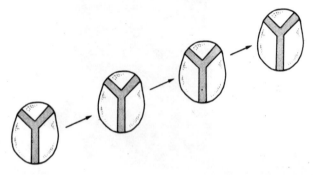

These are but a few of the ways in which transformations can be observed in patterns which are well within the scope of young children, and teachers will be able to think of many other examples. The value at this stage is in the observation of pattern and symmetry, and in the discussion on how the shapes were moved to produce the result.

Covering a surface area

One aspect of covering a surface has already been discussed in this section. This was fitting tiles together to introduce the idea of symmetry, and it can now be extended to bring in the first ideas of area as measurement of surface covered, or the amount of surface which a shape has, and that this is an approximate measurement. Before activities on measurement of area are attempted, teachers should make a test or check on the children's understanding of this idea. A suggestion for this is given below.

You will need two identical sheets of paper, and a dozen 1-inch wooden cubes. Place the two sheets of paper on the table a few inches apart. Tell the child the sheets represent two fields of grass. There are two farmers, and each has one field. Each farmer begins to build farm buildings on his field. Place one cube on each paper, then a second and a third. On one sheet place the cubes close together, on the other sheet scatter the cubes over the paper.

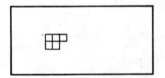 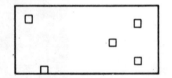

Tell the child each farmer has a cow. Ask the child whether the two farmers have the same amount of grass for their cows to eat. If the child says yes, continue to put buildings on each farm, always putting the same number of cubes on each sheet. Keep the cubes close together on one farm and scattered on the other, e.g.

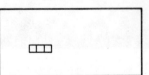 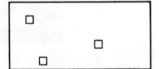

Again ask whether the farmers have the same amount of grass for their cows or not. If he still says yes, ask him why he is sure. If he replies that the farmers started with the same grass, that they have the same buildings and therefore the same grass left (or words to convey this idea) he has grasped the concept.

These lino-prints done by nine-year-old children show 'translation'.

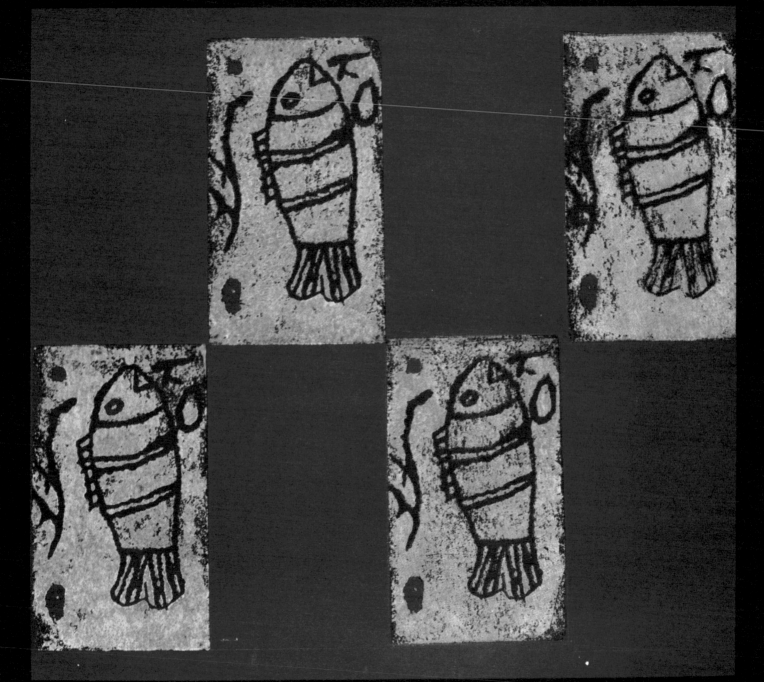

When children reach this stage, activities can be introduced which give experience in comparing the area of surfaces by the amount of surface covered. Home-made units and a variety of shapes will be used for this.

Assignments

Provide sets of geometrical shapes made of plastic material or card. These should include squares, rectangles, regular triangles, regular hexagons, regular pentagons and circles, with a sufficient number of each of the same size to try to cover the surfaces to be investigated.

> Take all the triangles. Estimate how many you will have to use to cover the front of the large reading book. Then use the triangles to cover your book. How many did you use? Was your estimate too big, or too small?

Repeat with the other shapes, i.e. use only circles, hexagons, rectangles, and so on.

> With which of these shapes did you find you could cover a surface?
> Which were not very good for this purpose?
> Write about this in your own way.

Compare the area (amount of surface) of various shapes using a grid, e.g., chicken wire. This has spaces roughly hexagonal in shape. Table mats, postcards, books, any flat objects with an interesting irregular shape are useful for this work.

Children might be set this task:

> Take three of these shapes. Use the wire netting to find which has the biggest surface on one side. Tell your teacher how you did it and write and draw about it.

This is the time to discuss with the children the various ways of covering a surface they have used so far. For example, 'Let's look at all the things we've used for finding which of these has the biggest area.' (Triangles, squares, circles, wire netting, etc.). 'Which do you think were useful?'

Discussion should lead to the idea of using squares, triangles and regular hexagons; and why pentagons and circles are not as useful. By analogy with the use of the cube for three-dimensional space, the square is probably the most useful. At this stage areas will be measured by the number of standard squares required to cover them and estimates must be made of the odd bits at the boundary of the surface covered. Children may well suggest taking two odd bits which together would seem to have just about the same area as the standard square; alternatively, they could get a reasonable approximation by ignoring the 'small' odd bits and counting the 'large' ones in as if they were each covered by a standard square.

Some assignments using squares can now be given.

Provide some tracing paper marked in squares ($\frac{1}{4}$in, 1cm, or 1in will do).

> Cover the front of your book with the squared paper and find how big it is by counting squares. Now do the same on a different book cover. Which was bigger? How do you know?

> Use graph paper marked in $\frac{1}{4}$-in, 1-cm or 1-in squares in a similar way. Trace round regular shapes and compare areas. Then try comparing the areas of irregular shapes such as leaves, using the square grid on the tracing paper.

When a group has done this discuss with them what to do with the bits of squares round the edges of the shapes.

AREA ~ 6 SQUARE INCHES

LEAVES

21 sq ins

16 sq ins

6 sq ins

4 sq ins

Linda   Holt

We had some leaf shapes and
drew round them on squared
paper. The squares were ½ inch
squares. We found that four
½ inch squares made the same
as a 1 inch square.

After drawing round them we
cut the leaves out. We
counted the squares remebering
that four small squares made a

one inch square.

4 sq ins

Children age 7 and 8
years

Publications of the Nuffield Mathematics Project:

Introductory Guide
●■▼ I do, and I understand   (1967)

Teachers' Guides
■ Pictorial Representation   (1967)
▼ Beginnings   (1967)
● Mathematics Begins   (1967)
❷ Graphs Leading to Algebra   (1969)
▼ Shape and Size   (1967)
❷ Computation and Structure   (1967)
❸ Graphs Leading to Algebra   (1973)
▼ Shape and Size   (1968)
❸ Computation and Structure   (1968)
▼ Shape and Size   (1971)
❹ Computation and Structure   (1969)
❺ Computation and Structure   (1972)

Weaving Guides
◯▯▽ Desk Calculators   (1967)
◯▯▽ How to Build a Pond   (1967)
◯▯▽ Environmental Geometry   (1969)
◯▯▽ Probability and Statistics   (1969)
◯▯▽ Computers and Young Children   (1972)
◯▯▽ Logic   (1972)

Check-up Guides
Checking up 1 (1970)
Checking up 2 (1972)
Checking up 3 (1973)

Other publications
The Story So Far   (1969)
Into Secondary School   (1970)
Problems – Green Set   (1969)
Problems – Red Set   (1970)
Problems – Purple Set (1971)
Maths with Everything   (1971)
Guide to the Guides   (1973)

For parents: Your Child and Mathematics   (1968)

The material in this book is taken from the Nuffield Guides:
● Mathematics Begins
▼ Beginnings
■ Pictorial Representation
❷ Computation and Structure
▼ Shape and Size

and has been selected and arranged by Mrs E M Williams, CBE.
Contributors to the original Guides included J W G Boucher,
G B Corston, H Fletcher, Miss B A Jackson, D E Mansfield
and Miss B M Mogford.